IMAGES
of America

BUCKS COUNTY

Touring bucolic Bucks County by car was as much a pastime in days gone by as it is today. Here George Weidner, Bertha Dietrick, Will Goldsmith, and Jean Reed pose along a county road in front of a split-rail fence typical of the time. (Courtesy of the Quakertown Historical Society.)

On the cover: This photograph was taken in the vicinity of the 1842 Pine Valley Covered Bridge on Pine Run Creek, New Britain. Seen here from left to right are H. Parmalee Burkart, Esher Claflin Burkart, Doris Miller, Clarence Miller, and Edwin Howard Burkart Jr. (Courtesy of Bruce Burkart.)

IMAGES
of America

BUCKS COUNTY

Kathleen Zingaro Clark

ARCADIA
PUBLISHING

Published by Arcadia Publishing
Charleston, South Carolina

Library of Congress Catalog Card Number: 2006921433

For all general information contact Arcadia Publishing at:
Telephone 843-853-2070
Fax 843-853-0044
E-mail sales@arcadiapublishing.com
For customer service and orders:
Toll-Free 1-888-313-2665

Visit us on the Internet at www.arcadiapublishing.com

Buckingham's Tyro Hall Grange, organized in 1912, has since merged with Plumstead Grange. This building was dedicated on November 12, 1932. According to Grange historical retrospectives, Granges began post–Civil War "for the economic, educational and political betterment" of farmers and helped bring mail service and electricity to rural areas, improve roads, and "facilitate other matters benefiting farmers and the nation." Several Bucks Granges remain active today. (Courtesy of Glenn Dutterer.)

CONTENTS

ACKNOWLEDGMENTS

The images in this book were compiled through the efforts of many individuals (and organizations too numerous to mention) to whom I extend my deepest appreciation.

Foremost, my gratitude belongs to the following: my husband, Roger Clark, for his unwavering support; my editor, Mary Ullman, whose assistance while combating the extreme physical adversity of multiple sclerosis made her contributions especially valued; and those who generously provided me both photographs and significant personal time, including Charles W. Lauble Jr., Gladys Koder, Nancy Roberts, Edwin Harrington, William Harr Sr., Elizabeth Luff, Sally Sondesky, Warren Williams, and Bruce Burkart, whose beautiful family photograph graces the book cover.

Equally important are others who shared images from personal or archival collections and helped caption: Don Haefner, Hilary Krueger, Marilyn Becker, Mary Jane Sergeant, Doug Crompton, Thomas Moll, Richard Mindler, Roger Lewis, Esther Smith, Barbara Stires, Cathy Thomas, Dave Drinkhouse, Gerald Taifer, Victor and Phyllis Teat, William Yerkes III, John Yerkes, Jim and Jane Murray, Birgitta Bond, Evelyn Griga, Harold and Carol Mitchener, Glenn Dutterer, Mickey and Ken Hicklin, Mira Nakashima-Yarnall, John Hoenstine, Jan Hench, John Chism, Jerry Forest, Maynard Cressman, Nellann Acevedo, Marge Blessing, Scott Blessing, Pamela Varkony, Ann Marie Bedeaux, Earl Davis, Ina Harmath, Michael Naylor, William Quigley, Rev. Sandra Reed, Dennise Veasley, Tim Rick, Clayton Fox, William Hall, Mary Stahr, and Kathryn Auerbach.

The following get credit for excellent leads or ideas: Franca Warden, Lyle L. Rosenberger, Florence Wharton, Carol Front, Margaret Capozzolo, Carla Foy, Betty Lou Painter, John Moore, John Reinhardt, Maureen McGonagle, Deanna Mindler, Dan Brashers, Murrie Gayman, Harriett Black, Lee and Kathie Poore, and Wendy Ringenary.

Friends and family offered encouragement and help, such as the critical technical support provided by Barbara Zlotnik and John Whalen, while these others expended time and effort on my behalf: Jo Ann Whalen, Roberta Trail, Debbie Oxman, Karyn Greenstreet, Joan Merkel, Marvin and Mayme Foral, Jennifer Brittingham, Betty Gannon, Marsha Hallett, Tom Hadderman, Doris Madara, John Kozlosky, Nancy Andal, Alice Krewson, Judy Brunner, Pam Sabutis, Kingdon Swayne, Bertha Davis, Michael D. Sherbon, Cindy Glick, Kathleen Meier, Audrey Adams, Tina Weber, Sue Kleiner Grew, Janet Prior, Pamela Corey, Cassandra Gunkel, Louise Davis, Vance Bachman, Ron Trauger, John Armstrong, Stephen Willey, Barbara Williams, Barker Gummere, Raymond Fox, Jim and Marty Steeley, Jim Pritchard, Sidney Taylor, Janet Braker, David Chavous, Walter Jacobs, Susan Bernstein, Richard Helm, Tony Blanchard, Jim Flannery, Jackie Schneck, Sara Burns, Dino Borghi Sr., and Bob Hunsicker.

I thank you all.

INTRODUCTION

To fully explore the history of Bucks County, one would need several years of serious study and more than a few seasons to meander. Yet the nostalgic images within this book help convey both the story and spirit of a region that encompasses over 30 historic districts on the National Register of Historic Places.

The abundance of Bucks County was well known to the Lenni Lenape Indians, who especially enjoyed meadow, river, and creek-side locales for their seasonal encampments and fishing expeditions. John Heckewekder, a missionary among them, once said, "They would rather lie down themselves on an empty stomach than have it said . . . they neglected their duty by not satisfying the wants of the stranger, the sick or the needy." And so the earliest 17th-century Europeans who forged into the back country were frequently aided in their survival by these magnanimous people.

In 1681, King Charles II of England granted Pennsylvania's founder William Penn a mass of woodlands destined to become America's fifth most populous state. Three counties, including Bucks, were formed within a year. Although a significant portion was partitioned to create Northampton County in 1752, there remained in Bucks more than 600 square miles of fertile land, harvestable woods, navigable waterways, and valuable natural resources to help build an important part of our nation.

Members of the Society of Friends (Quakers), enticed by Penn's promise of religious freedom, were among the first English-speaking people to make their way across the Atlantic into Bucks County. Overshadowing the Dutch and Swede traders who briefly settled the lower Delaware Valley in the 1600s, "they lived, improved their farms, increased in population and quietly gathered to their fathers" for several generations. In time, people of other nationalities, religions, and political persuasions settled around them and moved further into the county. The Dutch, Scotch-Irish, and Welsh initially settled the lower and central regions, while the Germans (Pennsylvania Dutch) moved principally to upper sections where they solidly retained their language and customs into the late 19th century.

Belts of limestone through the central and northeastern regions enriched thousands of acres of farmland and stoked the Durham Furnace, which smelted iron ore from the nearby hills. Moving along the Delaware River and canal from Easton to Philadelphia, rafts and Durham boats transported lumber, "Lehigh coal," and iron ore to build and sustain one of the world's greatest cities. As the river gave rise to commerce, shad fisheries, and steamboats, the Neshaminy, Tohickon, and other significant creeks continued to irrigate and drain the productive interior farmlands and power countless mills anchored to their banks.

Although the county steadily grew, the populace was not without disturbance. The so-called "Walking Purchase," little more than a fraudulent land grab in 1737 by second-generation proprietors Thomas and John Penn, undoubtedly led to the terrors that touched the county through the French and Indian War. Less than a century later, thousands of Revolutionary War soldiers marched the roads and set up countryside encampments, as private homes were converted into officers' quarters and local houses of worship were appropriated to create makeshift hospitals for the sick and wounded.

The subsequent Civil War and its aftermath, however, sparked progressive movement, industry, and innovation. The stagecoach was replaced by the railroad, and by the end of the 19th century, trolleys and automobiles had arrived. While towns like Bristol, Quakertown, and Sellersville experienced growth by rail, bucolic Bucks became a popular destination for writers, artists, playwrights, and performers as a new century dawned and unfolded. By the mid- to late 20th century, Bucks County had become one of the fastest growing in the country, doubling in population from 300,000 in 1960 to 600,000 in the year 2000.

Today the 31 townships and 54 municipalities that make up Bucks include not only an appealing mix of rural communities and thriving towns, but important commercial and cultural centers, popular tourist hot-spots, and intriguing historical villages. Each place possesses its own treasure trove of proud-moment stories, time-honored citizens, and history worth exploring.

One

RURAL LIFE AND BEAUTY

Looking State road by Oppenlander home toward Coopersburg

This lush spot in Passer is identified by the notation on the postcard as "State Road by Oppenlander home—looking toward Coopersburg." Using her countrywoman resourcefulness, this lady made a curved tree branch into a fairly comfortable-looking seat! Emmanuel Oppenlander owned the home at 1208 State Road. Onontacto Orchards, a farm in the village, was the birthplace of the Schimmel Preserve Company, apple butter "specialists." (Courtesy of Gladys Koder.)

This view of the Weir Farm, Richboro, shows the vast amount of farmland in Northampton Township before development. Farming on this property began before the Civil War. Harold Weir operated it from 1925 to 1991, and also drove a produce truck route every Friday in Glenside, Willow Grove, and Hatboro. His son Harvey, a pilot and photographer, took this photograph in the early 1950s before being killed in a plane crash.

This quintessential little red schoolhouse is believed to be Salem School, referred to as "the Rocks," near Zion Hill in Rocky Valley, although a similar school existed in Springfield Township. Early in Upper Bucks history, few schools were officially named but rather evolved from local usage, causing some confusion for present-day researchers. (Courtesy of Gladys Koder.)

These apples, perfect for making cider, were harvested from an orchard located on the northern slope of Springtown below Martin Lane and owned by Carey Dull (pictured here about 1920). Dull farmed 76 acres and had a "huckster" (fruit and produce) route in South Bethlehem. The country's first cider apples came from a tree planted in Buckingham by Thomas Smith, an elder of Buckingham Friends Meeting. (Courtesy of Lenore Ruth Schmoyer and Gladys Koder.)

Making apple butter required patience, attention, and a lot of help. Here Jennie Lauble and her helper stir the mix, cooking in copper pots with long wooden paddles. This all-day chore took 8 to 10 hours of constant stirring to complete. (Courtesy of Charles W. Lauble Jr.)

In this idyllic view of Springtown, a Quakertown and Eastern Railway locomotive puffs its way east. Abraham Funk founded Springtown after he purchased 300 acres from Stephen Twining in 1763. Funk built a mill eventually operated by several generations of his prominent descendants; it still stands on Cook's Creek. The family also published the *Springtown Times* newspaper for over 30 years, from 1886 to 1918. (Courtesy of Gladys Koder.)

The Delaware is the longest free-flowing river east of the Mississippi and is shown here at Riegelsville. Researcher John Garber found evidence that "mounds, trails, clearings, and abundant stone-paved fire sites" once extended from the Riegelsville Bridge to Durham Creek. This record of early occupation was destroyed by a freshet (spring thaw) in 1841. Paper and glass mills followed Riegelsville's early saw- and gristmills in the 19th century. (Courtesy of the Historic Langhorne Association, Ed Vogenberger Collection.)

This post office, pictured around 1913, was located on Durham Road south of Old York Road. The Buckingham Post Office was established in 1872, although an earlier one existed for the township at Holicong. Reportedly called Snaptown after a "surly and snappish" resident in the early 19th century, the town was identified as Buckingham by pre-Revolutionary maps. It has also been known as Bogarts Tavern, Vanhorns Tavern, Wilkinsons Tavern, and Centreville. (Courtesy of Jerry Forest.)

Greeting the mailman was an anticipated part of the day. Rural free delivery to farmers and rural residents began around 1900, although personal mail delivery had been recorded as early as 1802 in Bucks County. Legend states that Doylestown's first postmaster, Charles Stewart, stored the mail in his high beaver hat and hand delivered it during his walks about town.

High Falls in Bridgeton Township is a scenic feature of the area with a 30-foot drop into Falls Creek. The intriguing Ringing Rocks nearby are known for producing unusual musical qualities when struck. The northeast part of the township borders the Delaware River from Narrowsville (where cliffs were said to block direct sunlight in some places several months of the year) to Upper Black Eddy. (Courtesy of the Historic Langhorne Association, Ed Vogenberger Collection.)

Whenever the pond was cleared for ice-skating by this farmer and his Oliver tractor, it generated great excitement among the children of Negro League member William Teat, who lived across the road in the 1950s. This pond was located on the John Price Jones estate just above the Pineville Tavern. Built in 1742, the tavern was once the site of many public sales of livestock, equipment, and land. (Courtesy of Victor and Phyllis Teat.)

14

Corn shocks standing in the field were a common sight at harvest time when corn was cut and left in bundles to dry. Later each ear of corn was manually picked and stored in corn cribs and silos to be used as animal feed for chickens, pigs, and horses. Corn for the market and family was picked delightfully fresh. This child is Charles William Lauble, the father of Historic Langhorne Association historian Charles Lauble. (Courtesy of Charles W. Lauble Jr.)

This 1802 octagonal or eight-square schoolhouse in Wrightstown is a rare survivor among approximately 100 built in the Delaware Valley between 1800 and 1840. Its architectural design placed windows on each wall, maximizing light for students seated around a central stove. This schoolhouse was built of stone and is the last one of its kind in Bucks County. (Courtesy of the Historic Langhorne Association, Ed Vogenberger Collection.)

This "Dead Stock" removal cart says it all. (Courtesy of Gladys Koder.)

This romantic view of the canal bridge just below New Hope makes it seem worlds away from the hustle and bustle of the active tourist town today. The beauty of the canal, as evidenced in this photograph, is a magnet for lovers—locals and tourists alike. (Courtesy of the Washington Crossing Historic Park, Pennsylvania Historical and Museum Commission.)

The Geissinger Farm, just outside Pleasant Valley, was built by German settlers. A building of this size could easily shelter 15 to 20 cows and 2 teams of horses, as well as store tons of hay, wheat, or straw, several wagons, and farm equipment. The barn was destroyed by fire on January 27, 1911, although the house still stands. (Courtesy of Gladys Koder.)

It was common in the country to use oxen to pull logs, especially during Colonial times when virgin forests needed to be cleared for farmland. Ideally suited for the job, these draft animals were better able than horses to pull heavy loads and sustain long distances, particularly in cold weather. (Courtesy of the Historical Society of Bensalem.)

Ingham Spring, also known as Great Spring, in New Hope was called Achewetong by the Lenni Lenape Indians, who favored it as a camp area along their trail. James Logan, William Penn's secretary, was granted 500 acres of the Great Spring tract in 1702. Discharging three million gallons of water each day, the spring was able to provide the necessary power to run several mills in the 18th and 19th centuries.

Built in 1787, the Holland Mill received its power from the Iron Works Creek and abutted the Rockville (Holland) Covered Bridge. The gristmill here was known for many years as Finney's Feed Mill, named for the Finney family, who owned and operated it during the 19th and early 20th centuries. For a time, it was also called the Rockville Mill, a reference to the rockiness of the nearby creek banks. (Courtesy of the Historic Langhorne Association.)

Haupt's Mill, situated between Springtown and Durham, was one of four mills started in this vicinity on Durham Creek in the 18th century. It was purchased by John Haupt Sr. in 1757 from John Zigafuss, who built another mill nearby but abandoned it after losing a water rights dispute. Among the mills that operated here was a successful "oil mill," in which flax seed from Bucks and Northampton Counties was processed into animal feed. (Courtesy of Carol Dorey and Gladys Koder.)

Mary Miller, visiting from Philadelphia, and her children, Clarence and Doris, enjoy an outing at Pine Run Creek near the 81-foot Pine Valley Covered Bridge in southeastern New Britain Township. This bridge was built of hemlock in 1842. Early residents said the amount of white pine was plentiful, giving the stream and nearby village the name Pine Run. (Courtesy of Bruce Burkart.)

The Hulmeville Dam was built over the Neshaminy Creek in 1800 and was designed to control water flow to the cotton mills. Dutch settlers attempted to destroy the dam because it prevented shad and herring from migrating upstream. Here Elizabeth Blessing (Lizzy Schneider) sits nearby over 100 years later while the water gushes past her. (Courtesy of the Hulmeville Historical Society.)

Carversville General Store, built in 1910, was where locals might buy anything ranging from fresh produce, dried fruits, and canned goods to axes, shovels, and knickknacks. Although it was common for a village post office to reside inside the general store, mail could be collected here for just a short period of time. William Mitman stands in the center of this 1918 photograph.

The Pleasant Valley Feed Mill, erected by Paul Apple in 1805 in the center of the village, was subsequently operated by the Yosts—first Franklin, then his son Howard. It continued to serve area farmers into the late 1960s and early 1970s. According to local lore, General Lafayette stopped at the nearby Pleasant Valley Inn while en route to Bethlehem for medical treatment after he was wounded at the Battle of Brandywine. (Courtesy of Gladys Koder.)

This beautiful farm scene was common throughout the region a century ago. Today such beauty may still be found in abundance in Bucks County despite increased development and significant population growth over the past 50 years. (Courtesy of the Quakertown Historical Society.)

Contour farming, as seen in this aerial view of Yerkes farm, Furlong, was a conservation method introduced to stop erosion. Strips 85 feet wide followed the contour of the land and alternated between open and tilled ground for corn and sod crops such as clover hay. (Courtesy of John Yerkes.)

Raking hay seems to be a family affair on the Springfield Township farm depicted in this early-20th-century photograph. After it was gathered, the hay was stored in the barn and used as feed for dairy cows and work horses. It was also used agriculturally for seed retention and soil containment. (Courtesy of Gladys Koder.)

Washing milk cans was a daily chore necessary to eradicate bacteria before reuse. After milking the cows into small buckets, a farmer poured the milk into larger cans, which were stored in the springhouse. Chilled underground water would keep the milk fresh up to five days for family use. Industrious homemakers would use the excess milk to make cottage cheese and puddings rather than lose it to spoilage. (Courtesy of Charles W. Lauble Jr.)

Excess harvest from Bluledge Farm's apple orchard in Haycock Township is offered for the taking on Old Bethlehem Road in the 1940s. A family member, Pamela Feist Varkony, recalls that "money never changed hands between friends and neighbors" back then. Similar benches filled with honey, flowers, or canned goods were commonly offered for barter or sale into the 1960s. Surprisingly one may occasionally still encounter produce stands with "money jars" along area back country roads today. (Courtesy of Pamela Feist Varkony.)

In this c. 1930s aerial view of Newtown, Newtown-Yardley Road passes above the Newtown Cemetery, which is seen lower center, to the right of town. The roads running perpendicular to it in the upper left are Eagle Road (far left) and Washington Crossing. They are connected by Durham Road. A harness racetrack no longer in existence appears on the right. (Courtesy of the Historic Langhorne Association.)

A lady tends her garden in a country setting in one of many Bucks County images captured by early-20th-century photographer Newton Arnold. Newton and his brother Charles Arnold converted these images to postcards that are still enjoyed by collectors and history buffs alike. Note the root cellar in front of the ivy-covered house. (Courtesy of Warren Williams.)

This nostalgic image is of Funk's Mill, built in 1769 by Abraham Funk, Springtown's founder. Note the grain weighing scale and speeding train (left of center). The previous owner, Stephen Twining, among the earliest known settlers in the region, built the first mill here in 1738. The muddy road in the forefront is old Route 212. The current intersection of Routes 412 and 212 is above the train. (Courtesy of Gladys Koder.)

Work is play when you are helping a favorite aunt. Ina Hinkle Harmath helps her great-aunt Alice Myers of Plumstead dig a vegetable garden. Alice was a supervisor at the Keller Glove factory and one of the first in the community to purchase a television. Ina went on to work as a secretary at the Penn State Cooperative Extension of Bucks County for 38 years. (Courtesy of Ina Harmath.)

Emma Koder was baptized in 1918 in Springtown's Mill Creek by Reverend Mousley of the Christian Missionary Alliance. She later served as a missionary in India and lived to 104 years of age. Emma belonged to a congregation that worshiped in a small red church on Main Street (now a private residence) next to the original post office. Outdoor baptisms like hers were common in times past. (Courtesy of Gladys Koder.)

A woman and child peer from a tiny window overlooking the water wheel at this abandoned mill. Several dozen mills, most commonly lumber and gristmills, once existed throughout the county. Also in the area were horse-powered sorghum mills producing sugar and molasses, fulling mills making woolen cloth, and at least one large cotton mill. (Courtesy of the Quakertown Historical Society.)

Two

TRAVEL AND
TRANSPORTATION

School buses such as this one, transporting the National Farm School football team about 1920, were forerunners of the familiar yellow school bus launched in 1939, when national standards were established. In the late 19th century, the Wayne Works made horse-drawn carriages variously called school cars, school hacks, kid hacks, and school trucks. These horse-drawn school carriages served mostly rural students, including those in Bucks County. (Courtesy of the Delaware Valley College Archives.)

Dunk's Ferry Hotel, Bensalem Township, dates to the 1780s, although a tavern is believed to have operated here as early as 1733. Dunken Williamson launched a ferry service to Beverly, New Jersey, near this location in 1678. Postmaster and New Jersey governor Andrew Hamilton later petitioned William Penn for a road from the ferry to the Kings Highway (now Route 13). The road approved for construction is present-day Street Road. (Courtesy of the Historical Society of Bensalem.)

Steamboat inventor John Fitch, a silversmith, made guns for the Continental Army until British forces destroyed his Trenton shop in 1776. He moved to Warminster and years later conducted his first steamboat experiment on a nearby millpond. Around 1786, a larger model was successfully launched on the Delaware River, where service was briefly offered before an impoverished Fitch gave up. The invention was later credited to Robert Fulton. (Courtesy of the Historic Langhorne Association, Ed Vogenberger Collection.)

Elwood Doran (1827–1890) and later his son William (1852–1930) operated a ferry service between Bristol and Burlington from 1851 to 1930, closing just before the Burlington–Bristol Bridge was completed. The original ferry was established about 1680 by the first landholder, Samuel Clift. The Dorans named their ferry boats after themselves. Elwood is likely the gentleman in the center. (From the collection of the Margaret R. Grundy Memorial Library.)

Steamer "Twilight" and Ferry Boat "Wm. E. Doran", Bristol, Pa.

This steamer and ferry boat at Bristol used the waterway to transport travelers to Philadelphia and New Jersey, respectively. Before telephones, even a short trip or holiday spent visiting generated a postcard home. On this 1910 card, Arthur Starr wrote home to Philadelphia on Memorial Day weekend, "Dear Mom and Pop. Having a lovely time allright. xx Arthur." (From the collection of the Margaret R. Grundy Memorial Library.)

The Point Pleasant Inn was beautifully situated between the Delaware River and Tohickon Creek and operated into the 1920s. Many prominent people, including presidents Grover Cleveland and William McKinley, stayed here, as well as members of the eminently wealthy Vanderbilt and Astor families. Evidence indicates a specialty of the house was planked shad. (Courtesy of Warren Williams; photograph by Newton E. Arnold.)

At the time this rear view of the Black Bass Hotel in Lumberville was published (before 1907), the lodging was being promoted by the establishment as an "ideal summer resort." The tavern dates back to the 1740s. It is a matter of record that during the Revolutionary War patriots were not welcomed by the proprietors, who had remained loyal to the Crown. Currently a restaurant and bed and breakfast, it is reported to have considerable ghost activity.

Haupt's Mill Covered Bridge, built in 1872, extended 107 feet over the Durham Creek on Haupt's Bridge Road near Haupt's Mill in Springfield Township. It was destroyed by arson in 1985. Another covered bridge in Springfield Township, Knecht's (also called Slifer's), sits along the route of the infamous 1737 Walking Purchase and is one of only a dozen covered bridges remaining in Bucks County. (Courtesy of Gladys Koder.)

These fellows at Quakertown's Red Lion Inn may have been workers of the tannery next door. The inn opened as McCoole's Tavern around 1748. It gained notoriety in 1799, when John Fries led a revolt (Fries Rebellion) over a window-glass tax, resulting in the forced detention here of three federal tax assessors. Today the McCoole's name is back, and after 250 years, boarders can still find accommodations. (Courtesy of Jan Hench.)

31

This milestone on Old Bethlehem Road in Springfield Township was along the Philadelphia–Bethlehem stagecoach route. It advised southbound travelers 44 miles remained to Philadelphia. Inexplicably in the 1940s, the milestone apparently rested in front of an old schoolhouse near Gallows Hill on Route 412 before returning to its present location. These markers were instituted by Benjamin Franklin, joint postmaster general during Colonial times, in order to set fair postal rates.

This New Britain toll house on Route 122 (now 202) was located at Almshouse Road (now Tamenend Avenue) and the State Highway (now Butler Avenue). In the late-1700s, tolls ranged from 1.5¢ to 2.5¢, although churchgoers passed for free. The home was built by Benjamin Mathews Sr. and was still occupied in the mid-19th century by three female descendants: Mary Priscilla, Sara, and another. (Courtesy of Bruce Burkart.)

Travel by stagecoach was rough, its spring suspension jolting passengers up and down along the bumpy roads. The advent of the Concord coach in 1827 brought a newly designed suspension that yielded a side-to-side swinging motion and a far more comfortable ride. Numerous inns throughout Bucks County provided stage stops, where local mail was delivered and passengers could take respite while horses were changed. (Courtesy of the Historical Society of Bensalem.)

Conestoga wagons were driven by a teamster wielding "a fine squirrel-skin or silk 'cracker' " over his team of horses, according to 19th-century writer Alice Morse Earle. Milford Township was the most important center for "whip-stock" making in the United States for almost a half century. A lighter-weight Conestoga wagon used to transport families was common in Pennsylvania until around 1860. This c. 1930s photograph from a Bucks County collection may have been taken at a Wild West show. (Courtesy of Gladys Koder.)

The 1884 Calhoun Street Bridge spans the river in the vicinity of the "Falls of the Delaware." Here Colonial-era travelers between Philadelphia and New York used Colvin's Ferry to cross the river and proceed with their journey on land. The Dutch West India Company operated a trading post nearby (within present-day Morrisville borough) from 1624 to 1627. This was the first European settlement in Bucks County. (Courtesy of the Historic Morrisville Society.)

In 1765, the Delaware House opened as George II Hotel in Bristol, Bucks's oldest borough and one of the oldest settlements in the country. Bristol, the county seat from 1705 to 1725, was one of only three market towns in Pennsylvania when incorporated in 1720. British and American officers of the Revolutionary War were entertained here, as were Lafayette and later traveling presidents Madison, Tyler, Fillmore, and Adams. (From the collection of the Margaret R. Grundy Memorial Library.)

Spring-fed drinking fountains and troughs were essential for travelers and their horses along dusty roads providing few public facilities. Dedicated to Faith, Hope, and Charity, this one was located at the foot of the hill to the north (west) of the village of Langhorne. It was provided as a community service along Durham Road (now Route 413) and was located just north of the twin bridges. (Courtesy of the Historic Langhorne Association.)

John Cornell of Northampton takes his buggy for a courting visit with his future wife Margaret Weiss. She was a seamstress who lived for months at a time in the home of her customer while making the family wardrobe. A horse used for daily transportation such as the one pictured required only a signal to return home. If so desired, the "driver" could sleep all the way! (Courtesy of Betty Cornell Luff.)

Bogart's Tavern, built pre-Revolution in Buckingham, was headquarters for Gen. Nathanial Greene, troop commander of the 1776 Battle of Trenton. A year earlier, the Bucks County Committee of Safety met here to organize armed opposition to British rule. Early recollections about this 1752 watering hole (presently an antique shop) include an "enormous old fireplace," a hand-carved banister, and a pond that at one time required the diversion of York Road. (Courtesy of the Historic Langhorne Association, Ed Vogenberger Collection.)

Horseback riding necessitated the split skirts worn by Bucks County relatives Florence and May Antrobus, seen here enjoying themselves in Europe, where May's husband Charles, a navy consular, attended business. Florence Antrobus, raised on Thompson Mill Road, worked as the chief clinic nurse of the operating rooms at Hahnemann Hospital for a number of years. She also served as the 1932–1933 president of the Hahnemann Nurses Alumni Association. (Courtesy of Esther Smith.)

The Spring Garden Covered Bridge, at 218 feet in length, once had the distinction of being among the longest in Bucks County. Built over the Neshaminy Creek in 1815, it was located on the border of Newtown and Northampton Townships, near a mill of the same name. As a result of a devastating flood in 1955, only the supports remain. (Courtesy of the Historic Langhorne Association, Ed Vogenberger Collection.)

The Logan House, so-named in the late 1820s, has been in operation in New Hope for over 275 years. Located near a ferry, it has been variously known as Coryell's, Beaumont's, Canby's Tavern, and the Old Ferry Tavern. The name Logan was in honor of Lenni Lenape chief Wingohocking, who had, in the early 18th century, traded names to symbolize "his esteem and eternal friendship" with James Logan, William Penn's secretary. (Courtesy of Warren Williams; photograph by Newton E. Arnold.)

More than 250 years old, the Mountainside Hotel stood across from two canal locks and was an important respite for rafters transporting logs down the Delaware River for sale in Philadelphia. The area near Point Pleasant was "reputed to be one of the best fishing resorts on the river," and therefore many vacationed here, including Pres. Grover Cleveland. The building still exists in an area formerly known as Lower Black's Eddy. (Courtesy of the Historic Langhorne Association, Ed Vogenberger Collection.)

This 1916 Pine Valley Covered Bridge photograph shows just how rural the area was at the time. The view looks north from Keely Avenue to Iron Bridge Road. Doylestown Township would be to the right and New Britain Township to the left. The entire area around this bridge is now densely developed. (Courtesy of Bruce Burkart.)

The Washington House in Sellersville was a bustling establishment in a town where half the residents worked in cigar manufacturing (using tobacco locally grown by German farmers). A tavern license was first issued here in 1753. It became an important rest stop for travelers on the Weekly Post Stage Line operating between Philadelphia and Bethlehem. The North Pennsylvania Railroad came to town in 1856 and purchased the building, adding a 40-foot bar and the six-story tower and cupola that remain today. Present-day patrons are amused to learn that a 19th-century guest was required to store his gun in one of the 20 drawers behind the bar before taking a room. (Courtesy of William Quigley.)

The Eagle Hotel, located at Routes 202 and 152, is now the site of Borghi's Restaurant. During Revolutionary times, the tavern and local village were known as Kungle's Tavern after keeper George Kungle. It was a stage stop on both the Philadelphia–Bethlehem and New York–Lancaster routes. After a 1903 fire, active community member Harry Kelly purchased the rebuilt Eagle, designed by Oscar Martin. (Courtesy of Marilyn Becker.)

This Lumberville covered bridge was constructed in 1856. The flood of 1903 destroyed the portion replaced by the steel span shown here. For several years in the mid-1940s, the bridge was closed due to safety concerns and was changed to a Roebling-built suspension footbridge in 1947. The span connects the hamlet of Lumberville with Bulls Island State Park in Raven Rock, New Jersey. (Courtesy of the Historic Langhorne Association, Ed Vogenberger Collection.)

These ladies posing in a buggy with the family dog are Mary Anderson of Carversville and her unidentified cousin from Philadelphia. Like many young women of the time who sought independence, this cousin was a boarder living away from home but under the watchful eye of adults from another family. The buggy was the primary means of moving about town in the early 20th century, before automobile ownership had exploded.

Travelers crossing the Mill Creek Covered Bridge, heading south on Bridgetown Pike, would soon reach the Buck Hotel, a stagecoach stop established in 1735. The bridge was built near the Eight Arch Bridge in Northampton Township in the 1830s and removed in 1938. Here Abe VanArtsdalen stands at the entrance. (Courtesy of the Historic Langhorne Association.)

Will and Jean Goldsmith join friends Mr. and Mrs. George Weidner for a Sunday ride in a touring car around 1909. The Weidners each wear the popular muslin driving coat called a duster, specifically designed for the unpaved road conditions of the day. Note the wide netting both women employ to keep their massively stylish hats from blowing away. (Courtesy of the Quakertown Historical Society.)

Horseless buggies such as these were introduced in 1908 by self-taught mechanic Henry Ford. Photographer George Weidner captured a flat tire incident with friend Fred Harley on the Canal Bridge in Raubsville. In the early days of driving, flat tires were common given the poor roads. Among the earliest car owners, these fellows may have, like others, purchased their fuel in five-gallon cans from the local blacksmith. (Courtesy of the Quakertown Historical Society.)

The Pleasant Valley Garage served up gas and also serviced Ford Model Ts. Calvin Bleam built it in 1920 with concrete blocks he made himself. (Courtesy of Gladys Koder.)

This attractive group poses with a Ford Model T, the first automobile built for the average citizen. Introduced in 1908 for $850, it could travel up to 45 miles per hour with a simple turn of a crank. In 1916, around the time this photograph was taken, the price dropped to $350, making the dream of owning a "Tin Lizzie" that much more realistic. (Courtesy of the Quakertown Historical Society.)

Backbreaking railroad work was laboriously performed by immigrants eager to carve out a new life. This Pennsylvania Railroad track being laid around 1890 is near the Trenton cut-off of the Penn-Central (now Amtrak) Railroad, Langhorne area. This track created a bypass around the "congested" Philadelphia area and was completed in 1892. This line also provided passenger service until 1903. (Courtesy of the Historic Langhorne Association.)

The Chalfont train station was an important service to the locals of this farming and milling town who headed to Philadelphia to sell hay, flour, milk, produce, and other goods. The station was built in 1910 after fire had destroyed the original one. Fires often occurred when a train started and its steam engine sent sparks flying. Both Chalfont and New Britain reported such occurrences. (Courtesy of Marilyn Becker.)

The Flying Dutchman, a flying school operated by the Flying Dutchman Air Service, began in 1927, the same year the world celebrated the first solo transatlantic flight by Charles Lindbergh. The airport was located at the southeast corner of Street Road and Hulmeville Road in Bensalem Township. (Courtesy of the Historical Society of Bensalem.)

A passenger steam train runs along Muscrat Road, south of Paletown Crossing, in Quakertown. From 1945 to 1949, it had served as a U.S. Mail Railway Post Office express train between Bethlehem and Philadelphia. The last passenger trains traveled through Quakertown in 1981. (Courtesy of Maynard Cressman.)

This 1898 image of the "Train at Cawley's" shows a resting Quakertown and Eastern Railway passenger car. It was most likely stopped near the large community picnic celebrating the railroad's arrival in Springtown. A curious farm boy looks on as train personnel, riders, and a traveling mutt pose for the camera. The train was commonly known as the Q&E and nicknamed "the Quick and Easy." (Courtesy of Gladys Koder.)

Harvey Funk's carrier, seen here holding little Jim Wood, was typical of mail delivery wagons at the beginning of the 20th century. Jim later went on to work for the U.S. Postal Service and his wife, Verna, once served as postmistress of Carversville.

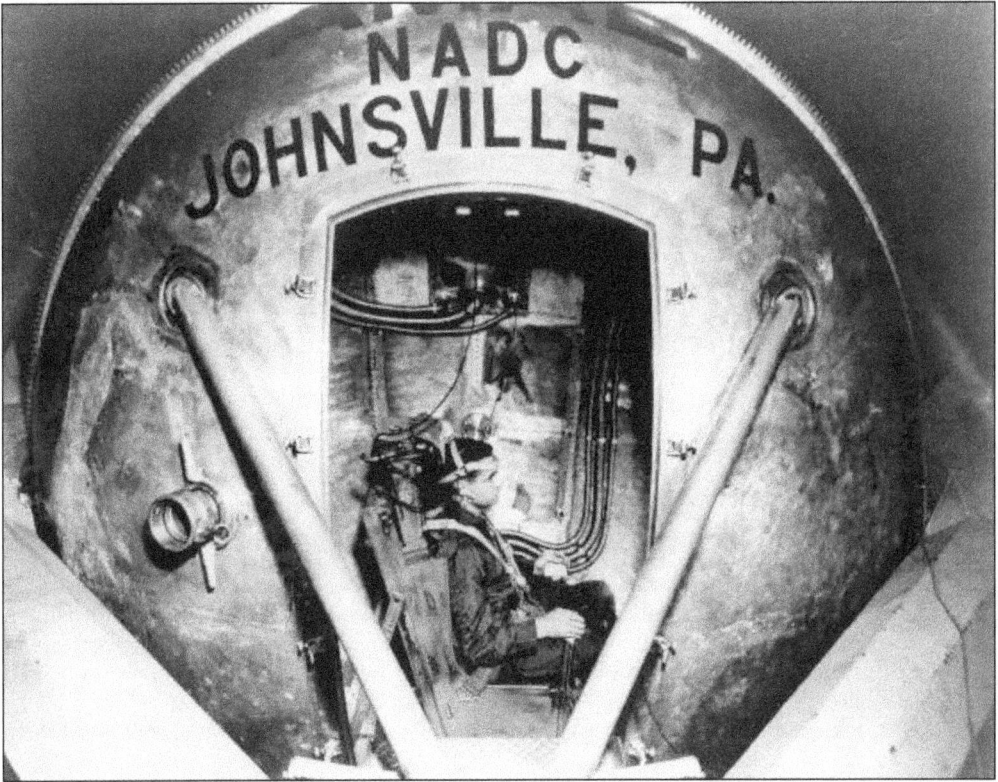

The Naval Air Development Center in Warminster was a designated United States training facility for early space programs, including the Apollo Mission. Astronauts John Glenn and Alan Sheppard received their training here on the first and largest human centrifuge built for that purpose. The facility was also used for testing modern aircraft, conducting naval air research, and developing weapons. (Courtesy of Doug Crompton.)

Children swarm a barnstormer after it lands in the field. Stunt pilots entertained the public at annual fairs and town events by executing daring maneuvers designed to evoke gasps of delight. Flying through and over barns was especially exciting and crashes were not uncommon. This plane may have left Setmans Airport, little more than a field in the Quakertown area of the 1920s–1930s. (Courtesy of the Quakertown Historical Society.)

Seen at Zion Hill, this Lehigh Valley Traction Company trolley operated between Philadelphia and Allentown on what became known as the Liberty Bell route, serving towns along Bethlehem Pike. The company was formed on November 17, 1899, when Albert L. Johnson consolidated his regional electric railway holdings. Although residents appreciated this convenient modern transport, track noise inflicted upon an otherwise quiet neighborhood was not as welcomed. (Courtesy of Gladys Koder.)

The Doylestown–Easton trolley, shown here in Plumstead, cost 95¢ for a one-way ride, which traveled 32 miles in two hours. The run was part of a scenic excursion route from Philadelphia to the Delaware Water Gap requiring six trolley changes. Passengers enjoyed magnificent views along the river and canal between Kintnersville and Easton. The trolleys were discontinued on Thanksgiving Day 1926, shortly after roads had been paved for automobiles. (Courtesy of William T. Hall.)

The unusual curved windows on this Duplex car were completely removable, converting it into an open-air trolley in the summertime. This photograph was taken about 1907 on Hellertown Avenue along the Quakertown–Richlandtown line, which launched on June 12, 1898. (Courtesy of the Quakertown Historical Society.)

Large farms required horse power for various activities in the old days. This woman used her horse simply to get around the property while performing a variety of farm chores. (Courtesy of Charles W. Lauble Jr.)

This spiffy gas station was part of the 72-acre Ridge Farm Motor Inn, a complex of campsites, rooms, and cabins in Bensalem Township on the original Lincoln Highway. In 1933, the state rerouted the road and moved the original building, a simple roadside stand, to this location aside the new highway. The owner then doubled its size and enhanced services, offering multiple brands of gasoline, as shown here. (Courtesy of the Historic Langhorne Association.)

These motorcyclists met at the Jitterbug on Route 309 near Broad Street in Quakertown during the early 1940s. The bikes shown here include six Indians and one Harley-Davidson. Moon Haney later opened a specialty barbecue business called Moon Haney's Pig Stand near this site on Park Avenue close to West Broad Street. (Courtesy of the Quakertown Historical Society.)

William J. VanMater's hauling truck sits in the alley west of the Susan K. Paxson House on East Marshall Avenue in Langhorne. Susan Paxson acquired the home when it was built in 1858 and lived there for 30 years. (Courtesy of the Historic Langhorne Association.)

A Greenwood Dairy truck is quite stuck in the muck on Reetz Avenue near Lincoln Avenue about 1936. The ice-cream window at Greenwood Dairy in Middletown Township was an exciting destination for farm and city folk alike. At the on-site restaurant, a colossal ice-cream sundae called a Pig's Dinner was offered with a prize pin announcing "I was a pig at Greenwood Dairy" for anyone who could devour the entire feast. (Courtesy of the Hulmeville Historical Society.)

This beautiful stone arch bridge was built across Cook's Creek in Pleasant Valley in 1777. It was the entry point to the area for immigrants and travelers along the "Great Road" from Philadelphia to Bethlehem, as well as a popular ice-skating site during the early 1900s. (Courtesy of Gladys Koder.)

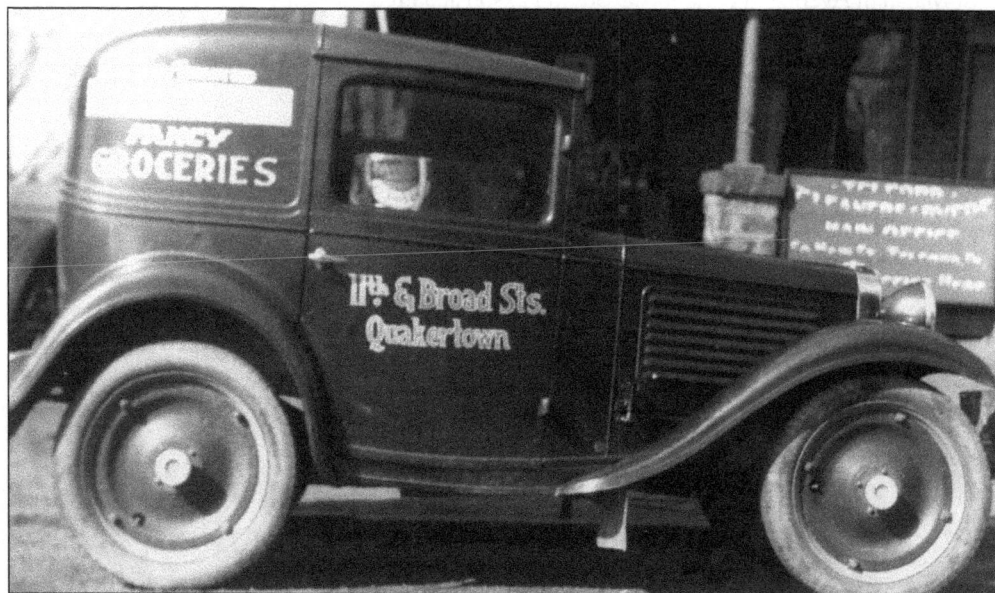

Neighborhood grocery stores were found in every town before the days of chain convenience stores. One of Quakertown's stores in the 1930s and 1940s was A. S. George's, at 11th and Broad Streets. Alfred George later closed the store ostensibly because of frustration with rationing requirements during World War II. His customers received free delivery of orders from this vehicle. (Courtesy of the Quakertown Historical Society.)

Bicycle explorations around the farm and along adjacent country lanes were exciting Sunday activities for the Lauble, Johnson, Stroup, and Harrison kids in the 1920s. While their mothers peeled potatoes and fathers pitched horseshoes before their big Sunday supper, this gang of cousins posing in front of the haycocks got to enjoy true country life. Pictured here from left to right are Charles Lauble, Zora Johnson, Russell Johnson, Althea Jones, Clara Lauble, and Edith Harrison. (Courtesy of Charles W. Lauble Jr.)

In the 1920s, Richland Township's public transportation began with the arrival of the first bus operating between Richlandtown, Quakertown, and Trumbauersville. Shown here is one of the first bus drivers, Mr. Biehn, in Richlandtown. The home behind the bus was owned by Frank Ahlum. (Courtesy of the Quakertown Historical Society.)

Something new in Holland since you left. 8, 10, 06 Grandma.

Spanning Iron Works Creek, the oak Rockville (Holland) Covered Bridge was built 139 feet long in 1830 and was removed just over 100 years later, in 1932. Covered bridges were often referred to as kissing bridges. After snowstorms these bridges were "snowed"; in other words, snow was shoveled into them to provide traction for sleighs and sleds. (Courtesy of the Historic Langhorne Association.)

Sleigh riding was an extremely popular wintertime activity. Sweethearts especially enjoyed sleighing frolics, rides in the moonlight, and the time alone a sleigh ride offered. Because of the low cost, middle-class families could more commonly afford sleighs than carriages. (Courtesy of Gladys Koder.)

54

Three

WORK AND PLAY

Old Beers Orchard in Rock Hill was later known as Charles N. Cressman's Orchard. Although not specifically identified, those captured in this 1899 photograph include James Otten Sr., Albanus Freed, Charles Boyle, Warren Biehn, and Charles C. Biehn. The rest are unknown. (Courtesy of the Quakertown Historical Society.)

Burlington Island Beach Park drew summertime visitors from Bristol, Burlington, New Jersey, and the surrounding region. Picnicking, boating, and swimming were enjoyed on the island from the end of the 19th century until 1934, when the park was destroyed by fire. An amusement park was added about 1917, and the YMCA held canoe races here. (From the collection of the Margaret R. Grundy Memorial Library.)

Bailing hay the old-fashioned way entailed using a stationary hay bailer, considered modern equipment around 1925–1935. Typically the hay was brought to the barn by hay wagons then manually fed into the bailer. Today mobile bailers do the job in the fields. (Courtesy of Charles W. Lauble Jr.)

Filling the silo at the National Farm School in Doylestown required intense labor by students, many of whom came from a comfortable city life. An early aim established by the institution was "to provide youths with a type of farm training, which would enable them, upon graduation, to engage in practical agricultural pursuits." (Courtesy of the Delaware Valley College Archives.)

Barge rides along the Delaware Canal and fishing on the towpath are activities still enjoyed today. Canoes, kayaks, and rowboats dot the waterway, while skating, biking, hiking, and picnicking enhance the experience of enjoying its beauty. The canal became public domain in 1932 after 100 years of commercial activity. It is now part of the Delaware and Lehigh National Heritage Corridor managed by the Department of Conservation and Natural Resources. (Courtesy of the Washington Crossing Historic Park, Pennsylvania Historical and Museum Commission.)

The Esser basketball team, sponsored by the Esser News Agency of Quakertown, played in Richland Township in the 1920s. It was common during the 1920s and 1930s for community businesses to sponsor sports teams and bowling leagues and buy the players' uniforms and jackets. (Courtesy of William Harr Sr.)

These Reading Railway employees worked on a section gang of three to five men responsible for maintenance and repair of train tracks. An unidentified man (left), Howard Ruth (center), and Ralph Kneller are seen here regauging the rails (correcting their width) south of the Fairview Crossing in Quakertown. (Courtesy of Maynard Cressman.)

Anna Funk sits at a spinning wheel in period costume demonstrating the craft of her ancestors. Until the early to mid-19th century, young women, especially among the Germans and Quakers, were trained to spin flax and wool into thread and yarn for making family clothes and linens. In most Colonial homes a whirring spinning wheel was the first thing one heard or saw upon entering the home.

Springfield High School baseball players pose for a photograph. Shown here, but not specifically identified, are Gwynetta Weirbach, Bill Frankenfield, Clyde Frankenfield, Hartford Benner, Walter Unangst, Horace Stover, Ira Frankenfield, Wilmer Fretz, P. Trumbore, and Frank Frankenfield. (Courtesy of the Springfield Historical Society and Gladys Koder.)

The S. P. Gillingham Company in Langhorne was a milk delivery business owned and operated by Sarah Gillingham. Home deliveries were common through the 1950s and are still made in parts the county today. Wives and daughters of dairy farmers often maintained routes, while others like Sarah Gillingham and Ida Cressman Unangst, who started a milk delivery route in Springtown in 1927 with her husband Raymond, were directly involved in the operation. (Courtesy of the Historic Langhorne Association.)

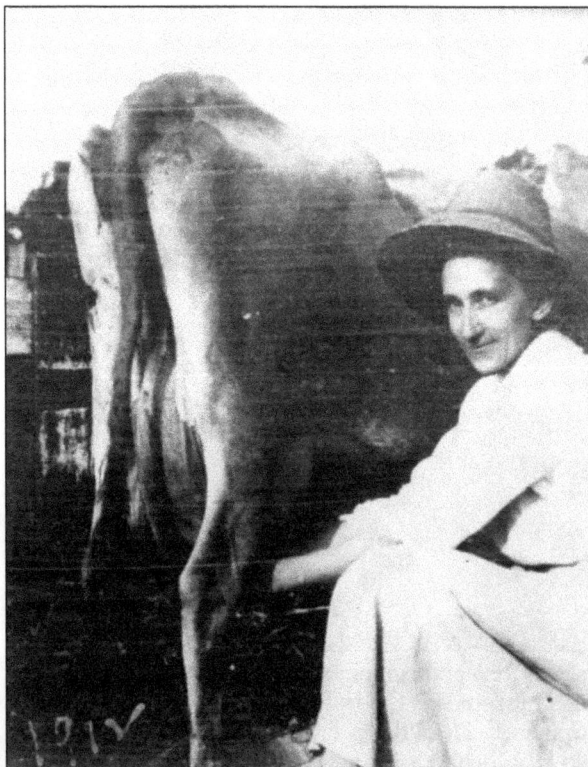

Milking the cow was a twice-daily chore usually assigned to the females of the family. Pictured here with her Jersey cow is Mary Anderson of Carversville. Mary organized sewing circles, once a popular pastime for women, in the community. Her husband, Josh, was a local auctioneer.

Shown here about 1925 is the dairy at the Northern Christian Orphanage in Carversville. These boys are at the Hillside barn, part of the dairy operation run by the orphanage.

This milk truck, pictured about 1920, transported raw milk to the Castanea distribution center in Trenton, founded by Henry Comfort of Falls Township. Milk was once considered "one of the most valuable products of the county," and although "butter making [was] still in the hands of farmers' wives" before 1879, the county contained 55 operating creameries before the end of the 19th century.

The Harriman Fire Department, seen in 1918, protected Bristol's Merchant Shipbuilding Corporation and the surrounding community of Harriman (named for shipyard owner W. Averell Harriman). The building was part of a business that manufactured 9,000-ton steel-hulled freighters for the federal government during World War I. Several soap companies, including Purex and Dial, later took up residence here. (From the collection of the Margaret R. Grundy Memorial Library.)

Third-generation boat captain Joseph W. Reed Sr. transported anthracite coal, used for heating, manufacturing, and cooking, down the 60-mile Delaware Division Canal from 1919 until 1931, when mule-driven boat service ended. His personal recollections include working many long, hard hours, liquor smuggling during Prohibition, and living on the barge with his family during the Depression, when his daughter (baby in arms) Betty Reed Meyer of Doylestown was born. (Courtesy of the Reed family.)

Francis O. Strouse started the Strouse Bakery Company in 1908 and operated it from this location in Springtown, delivering goods throughout the surrounding communities. After Strouse declared bankruptcy in 1913, Wilbert Frey ran the company until 1923. The baking ovens remain in place in a back section of the home. (Courtesy of Ruth Unangst Johnson and Gladys Koder.)

Picking apples the "Del Val" way provided firsthand experience to students in farm operations, as shown here. The horticulture curriculum also included the production, processing, and marketing of fruit and vegetable crops. (Courtesy of the Delaware Valley College Archives.)

A man visiting Emery Cox's Barber Shop enjoyed camaraderie with each haircut and shave. Every customer had his own shaving mug on the wall. The shop was located in Morrisville, where a "Gray Stones" marker designates the origin for all land surveys conducted in Pennsylvania after William Penn first purchased land from the Lenni Lenape in 1682. (Courtesy of the Historic Morrisville Society.)

Roberts and Browning Tin Shop, also known as Schatt's, at 231 Main Street in Hulmeville sold and repaired heaters, ranges, kettles, coffee pots, utensils, and other tinware. Tinsmiths typically supplied these goods in addition to down spouts and tin roofs. This c. 1895 photograph includes, from left to right, Erda, Susan, Tom, Daniel, and Billy White, with Anna the horse. (Courtesy of the Hulmeville Historical Society.)

Boaters and friends gathering at Dewey (Hulmeville) Park about 1900 include "Shiner" Walton (number 8, seated left) and Otto Schoenfeld (number 7, seated right). In 1898, Charles Haefner and Hulme Harrison purchased the Harrison farm property to create a picnic grove with a dance pavilion, refreshment stand, and swimming area on the Neshaminy Creek. Later the pavilion became a roller-skating rink and the park a popular resort when summer cottages were added. (Courtesy of the Hulmeville Historical Society.)

This group feverishly packed from 10:00 p.m. until 4:00 a.m. for dawn delivery to Philadelphia to ensure "dew fresh" corn was available to customers within 18 hours after its removal from the stalk. This well-received concept was started in the early 1950s by Buckingham farmer William Yerkes Jr. of None Such Farms and his partner Art Kinney. Pictured here from left to right are Maude Funk Large, Barbara Yerkes Mitchell, Betty Porter, and Sam Shenberger (stooping). (Courtesy of John Yerkes.)

H. S. Mill Cannery workers husked and canned corn, beans, and surplus produce brought in by local farmers. Remnants of the facility, including an old silo, remain today behind Springtown's only gas station. On July 30, 1904, the *Town and Country* newspaper reported a bean pickers' strike, noting that "the Cannery is kept running by uprooting the bean vines and picking the beans there from inside of the factory." (Courtesy of Gladys Koder.)

In this photograph, men camp beside an unidentified Bucks County stream near a steel bridge. It was among several unrecorded photographs found in a Newton Arnold collection after his death. Newton and his brother Charles published hundreds of Bucks County images as postcards in the early 20th century. (Courtesy of Warren Williams.)

Neshaminy Falls Park, near Oakford in Bensalem, was a popular recreation site for over 60 years beginning in 1876. A Bensalem publication noted this "miniature Coney Island" featured "a carousel, scenic railroads, fun houses, shooting galleries, wheel games, some side shows, tintype photography, motorboat rides, a roller skating pavilion, and a thirty-foot sliding board." Music, dancing, picnic tables, and hot air balloon demonstrations were added attractions that helped draw visitors by the thousands. (Courtesy of the Historical Society of Bensalem.)

Preparing cabbage for market or for sauerkraut was just one farm chore for Addie Strock, pictured here with a worker. Addie and her husband raised fruit and vegetables on their Funk Mill Road farm. Strock produce could be found at the Bethlehem Farmer's Market. (Courtesy of Gladys Koder.)

This truck hauls hay that will be used for multiple purposes on the farm, including feed for livestock and a cover for plants during winter to prevent a deep freeze. (Courtesy of the Historical Society of Bensalem.)

Economists get a lesson from herdsman Chester Raught, standing with the record-holding cow for milk and butterfat production at the National Agricultural College (now Delaware Valley College). The United Nations Bureau of Economic Affairs sponsored these visitors from Liberia, Tunisia, Guinea, Ghana, the United Arab Republic, Togoland, British Somaliland, Somalia, Ethiopia, and Libya as part of a 1960 international training effort for African government economists. (Courtesy of the Delaware Valley College Archives.)

These prize potatoes, grown by Charles F. Luff (on tractor), were originally stored, bagged, and weighed in his home's basement until a building was added for this purpose. Luff purchased his Lower Holland Road farm for $10,000 in 1914, when he married his sweetheart, Mary Fridell. Later his sons Albert and Vincent helped run the family farm. Vincent resided on the property with his wife, Betty Cornell Luff. (Courtesy of Betty Cornell Luff.)

Squirrel hunter Frank Wood may have used his rifle to take "pot shots" at squirrels on his own property or while out with friends pursuing this once-favorite sport. Squirrel meat, said to taste like chicken, is still included in recipes today.

Washing was just one chore for a farm woman raising a family. Besides being the household's seamstress, mother also had to "put up string beans, peaches, applesauce, corn, pickled beets, eggs, sauerkraut," and other produce that could be stored for the months ahead. This woman did her laundry using a wood-framed washboard made of either ridged metal or glass until the electric washing machine became a standard household appliance. (Courtesy of Charles W. Lauble Jr.)

Captured in a relaxed moment by Newton Arnold, Grenoble station master for 27 years, these laborers were likely among those preparing hay or lumber at the station for freight transport or else workers at the nearby quarry. Arnold and his brother published photographic postcards of Bucks County and surrounding areas in the early 1900s. (Courtesy of Warren Williams.)

The American Telephone and Telegraph Company had not yet monopolized the American market when Newton Arnold photographed theses workers hauling telephone poles in 1907 near the Grenoble station. Once the poles were erected, a series of insulated wires would be suspended between them to create a communications network. (Courtesy of Warren Williams.)

Ice-skating was a popular winter pastime on farm ponds and lakes throughout the county. A crowd on the lagoon at Washington Crossing Historic Park was quite common in the 1950s, when freezing temperatures created the right conditions for twirling and swirling across the ice. (Courtesy of the Washington Crossing Historic Park, Pennsylvania Historical and Museum Commission.)

The crowd at this 1920 Memorial Day parade in Morrisville was typical of such town events. Children were especially proud to participate in formation with their classmates. Parade marchers head down Washington Street just below Green Street. Murray's Store (upper left), as it was known during the Depression era, was operated by James A. Murray Sr., the father of Jim Murray, author and historian with the Historic Morrisville Society. (Courtesy of the Historic Morrisville Society.)

Boys at Kirks Corner School in Carversville look primed for a baseball game in 1927. The original school, built in 1794 by Buckingham Friends at Aquetong and Saw Mill Roads, stood across from former American Indian camping grounds and was replaced in 1861. Pictured here from left to right are (first row) Pearson Thatcher (note his beanie), John Worthington, Tony Siran, John Anderson, and Kenneth Foster; (second row) Jim Wood, Sid Michener, Leon Sine, Bob Paul, and George Matuski.

The Johnson family children of Richland Township learned to handle reins while at play with miniature pony Lizzie on the family farm. Clarence is on the far left and Alfred on the far right. The other children remain unidentified. Although Richland Township was known as the "Great Swamp" during Colonial times, the soil was actually quite fertile in this low-lying region. (Courtesy of Katherine Bean Landis and the Quakertown Historical Society.)

Devil's Half-Acre, consisting of a house and patch of land between the Delaware Division Canal and River Road near Lumberville in Plumstead Township, was reputedly a notorious watering hole for canal builders during the 1830s. Historian George MacReynolds reported that whiskey was sold without license from a stone building, perhaps the one pictured, and was the scene of much drunken revelry.

The United Cigar Manufacturing Company employed several boys who most likely left school to apprentice in the trade. Cigar making was once an important industry in Rockhill and Milford Townships. Hand-rolled cigars gave way to mechanization in 1919. By 1932, Bucks County manufacturers were producing over 11 million cigars annually. The "strippers wanted" sign refers to the task of stripping tobacco leaves from the stalk. (Courtesy of the Quakertown Historical Society.)

Established in 1911 (as the Eden Fire Company), the South Langhorne Fire Company poses with its 1921 American LaFrance Cosmopolitan fire truck after a parade at Hulmeville Park in the early 1930s. The fire company was renamed Penndel in conjunction with the borough name change in 1948. Shown here, from left to right, are the following: (first row) unidentified and Fred Hewins; (second row) Lawrence Devlin, unidentified, Perry Keating, Joe Lukens Sr., Leroy Devlin, Joe Camilla, Bill Hewins, Fred Dunkley, and Fred Bango. (Courtesy of Janet Wachtendorf and Katrina Orfe.)

The keg parties hosted by Joe Klein were legendary. Joe and his wife, Lydia Klein (née Benner) of Trumbauersville, operated Sellersville's Washington House from approximately 1905 to 1915. Although federal agents removed and demolished the saloon's bar during Prohibition, regular patrons reportedly continued to have their thirst quenched here. A new liquor license was issued on December 3, 1933, two days before Prohibition was officially repealed. A new bar was installed by June of that year. (Courtesy of William Quigley.)

Musical chairs was one of many enjoyable activities for visitors to Chalfont's Forest Park in the 1950s. The park attracted thousands of people from its beginning in 1885, including notables such as Harry Truman. It was a great place for picnicking, swimming, boating, dancing, amusements, and live entertainment. Richard and Elsie Lusse, manufacturers of amusement rides such as the bumper cars, were full owners of the park from 1942 to 1959. (Courtesy of John Mallack.)

These employees in Langhorne occupy one of many Reading Railroad Company stations designed by noted architect Frank Furness. It was built in 1881 for $2,693. Following a fire in January 1920, two passenger cars were lifted into place by derricks to serve as the ticket office and passenger waiting area until the present building was rebuilt and completed three months later. (Courtesy of the Historic Langhorne Association.)

This hose cart belonged to the Sellersville Fire Department, established in 1888, and was sold during the Depression to help raise funds. It is now included in the Philadelphia Firemen's Museum collection. Sellersville was known as Sellers' Tavern, after 18th-century tavern owner Samuel Sellers, until 1866. Incorporated in 1874, it had its own newspaper, the *Sellersville Herald, Independent in Politics*, by the end of the 19th century. (Courtesy of William Quigley.)

The Langhorne Brickyard sold its salmon-colored clay bricks to builders as "far away" as Bristol and "Bustletown" (Bustleton). These bricks were used to build Bristol's Delaware House. By the late 1800s, the yard was producing up to three million bricks annually. Although Langhorne was a residential community, a brick-making industry operated there from 1700 to 1930. Here women and children are turning the bricks so they will dry evenly in the sun. (Courtesy of the Historic Langhorne Association.)

Mandolin and violin players comprise this young student orchestra, which included a single horn player and a young lady vocalist. (Courtesy of the Quakertown Historical Society.)

Dating to the early 18th century, Yardley's Afton Lake is really part of a man-made water system of dams, canals, and ponds created to activate grist- and sawmills. *Benjamin Franklin's Gazette* mentioned it in 1731, but it was actually recognized in a deed earlier, in 1713. Supposedly a settler named the lake in honor of Scottish poet Robert Burns's work "Afton Waters." (Courtesy of Bruce Burkart.)

The youngest of 13 children, Lillie May Hinkle lost her mother, just 42 years old, to a typhoid fever epidemic that swept through Plumstead in 1913. Lillie's father, Frank W. Hinkle, was a lifelong tinsmith who did repair work at the homes of local families and maintained a shop adjacent to the 18th-century Plumstead Inn at Easton and Stump Roads, next to his own family home. (Courtesy of Ina Harmath.)

Strawberry pickers take a break on Jacob and Alice Greup's farm. An on-site butcher shop sold chicken and veal (a specialty). Greup's produce, butter, and eggs were sold locally and at the Bethlehem city market. In the front left is Preston Koder, grandfather of Gladys Koder, a Springtown Historical Society historian who has produced numerous pictorial calendars capturing Springfield Township's historical past. Jacob Greup is the mustached gentleman standing with the basket. (Courtesy of Gladys Koder.)

The 1916 all-star baseball team poses in front of the Red Lion Inn, Quakertown. The pitcher was "Lefty" Clemmer (not specifically identified in this photograph). According to a 1905 publication, the inn's patrons enjoyed "5¢ beer . . . sumptuous free lunches . . . and all you can eat dinners for 25¢" in appreciation for not giving their business to the nearby Eagle, Globe, Continental, or Bush House. (Courtesy of William Harr Sr.)

The Tohickon Stone Quarry was started in the early 1930s by Clyde Feist, who operated it until the late 1960s, taking great advantage of the trap rock that runs through Rockhill Township and forms Haycock Mountain. The 100-acre property produced crushed stone for construction purposes and included concrete and asphalt plants. The quarry was later confiscated under the rules of eminent domain and flooded to make Lake Nockamixon. (Courtesy of Pamela Feist Varkony.)

Horse-drawn hay rides have always been great fun, especially for these children from the Carversville Christian Children's Orphanage at Hillside Farm. Pictured here from left to right are Dan Barnhart (at reins), Mrs. Harry Meyers, Elva Meyers, unidentified baby, unidentified, Charles Pettit, unidentified, and Harold Dodd. The rest are unidentified.

Quakertown High School's first football team had a 7-4 record, beating every other team in Bucks County. Jake Stoneback served as coach. The team was reportedly formed in 1920; however, the fellows who played that year are not the same as those in this photograph, identified as Quakertown High's first team. (Courtesy of the Quakertown Historical Society.)

"Ring-a-Ring o' Roses" is a centuries-old nursery rhyme that inspired a charming children's game. Here Elizabeth Antrobus plays with her children Esther (now Smith) and Jim and friends in the front yard in the early 1920s. The family lived south of Bowman's Hill in the hamlet of Lurgan. (Courtesy of Esther Smith.)

Four

PEOPLE AND PLACES

Quaint farming couple William and Levina Heller Pearson lived in this log home in Danneltown (or Danieltown) near Stoney Garden and raised 14 children in the mid- to late 19th century. Henry C. Mercer, a founder of the Bucks County Historical Society, described the typical first home of a settler as a "rectangle of heavy logs" roofed with "bark or shingles" and caulked with "grass and clay." (Courtesy of Gladys Koder.)

Haycock Township's Stover School, located in an area once referred to as Stover's District, is now Cappie's Park Tavern on Route 563 at Old Bethlehem Road. The expansive 5,283-acre Nockamixon State Park is nearby. (Courtesy of the Richland Library Company.)

This gun-toting, car-stealing sextet was arrested in 1933 by Quakertown officers George Harr and Edward Shearer. They were overtaken after a 14-mile car chase that reached 80 miles per hour. These Philadelphia "youths," between the ages of 19 and 22, were found with a sawed-off shotgun, three revolvers, and a blackjack. (Courtesy of William Harr Sr.)

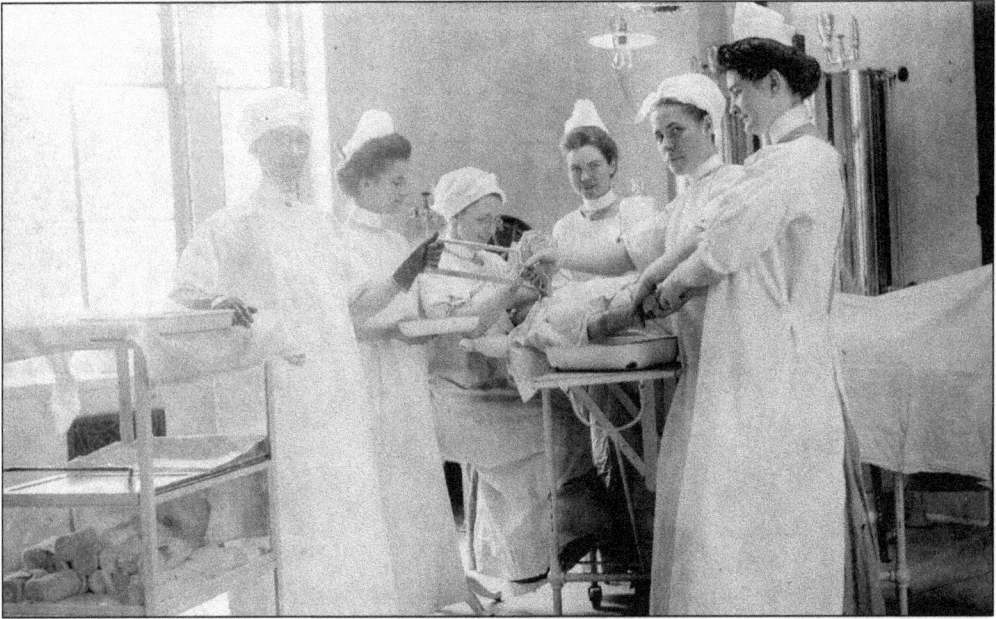

Gehman's Hospital, started in 1921 by 30-year-old nurse Emma Gehman (far left), provided emergency and maternity care to 1,100 people in the Quakertown region in the eight years under Gehman's management. This was purportedly the first operation performed at her facility. Gehman was given the honor of turning the first spade to break ground for the Quakertown Community Hospital, opened in 1930. (Courtesy of the Quakertown Historical Society.)

A Revolutionary-era gravestone in Bedminster Township reads, "In memory of Major William Kennedy who died of wounds he received from a robber on the first day of September in the year of our Lord 1783 in the 40th year of his life." Kennedy was killed during a raid on the Tohickon Creek hideaway of local horse thieves, robbers, and Tory raiders known as the Doan Gang.

This 1936 Memorial Day parade on Lincoln Highway in South Langhorne took place four years after the State Highway Department unveiled plans to upgrade the road into a new superhighway. A few years later, construction was abandoned, leaving a "road to nowhere." The project was revived in the 1960s and opened up rural communities to commercial development. (Courtesy of the Historic Langhorne Association.)

On Booster Day during World War I, Quakertown soldiers seem happy to pose for a photograph. Shown here from left to right are William W. Muelhauser, C. Norman Detweiler, Peter C. Romig, and Earle Ball. (Courtesy of the Quakertown Historical Society.)

This Spanish-American War soldier is W. T. Sherman Black, age 30 in 1898. The Black family was Mennonite and descended from immigrant Abraham Schwartze, who came from the Rhineland area of Germany. Several generations lived on Old Ferry Road in Plumstead. Over the years, many Schwartze family members changed their last name to Black to reflect the English meaning of their German name.

World War I Red Cross workers, in their caps and printed white dresses, join others for a community event, most likely a celebration on Armistice Day in 1918. Pictured here, in the front row from left to right, are Edith Michener Williams, unidentified, Kizzie Worthington, Lucile Walton, and Margaret Flack.

The Henry H. Wisler Memorial Baptist Home for the Aged, located at Main Street and Park Avenue in Chalfont, was purchased in 1917 by the Patriotic Order Sons of America. It supplemented a 72-acre farm acquired in 1907 for the needy of their order. In 1919, the original home became an orphanage, which housed 10 boys and 13 girls by 1924. The home reported 20 men and 13 women residents that same year. (Courtesy of Marilyn Becker.)

The Underground Railroad was a series of secret respite stations for runaway slaves. In Bucks County, it was supported principally by the Quaker community. This Quakertown home, owned by Richard Moore, a farmer and red-ware pottery manufacturer, was a stop. During the day, slaves found security in Moore's barn. At night, while well hidden under straw, they were taken farther north toward safety in his long pottery wagon. (Courtesy of the Quakertown Historical Society.)

The traditional Quaker garb worn by Julia Balderston was most likely donned for a 250th anniversary celebration at Newtown Friends Meeting in 1934. Earlier Julia had studied in Paris and was a suffragette. She taught school, traveled Europe, and worked as a guide for the Metropolitan Museum of Art in her later years. Julia also knew Woodrow Wilson well enough to be invited to his inauguration. She lived to age 106. (Courtesy of Esther Smith.)

Middletown Meeting, formed in 1683, offered Bucks County's "best school of the day" in the early 18th century, according to historian George MacReynolds. Overcrowding at the 1721 Quaker Meetinghouse (which had replaced a building erected in 1688) led to construction of this meetinghouse on Maple Avenue in 1793. Member growth led to the development of Langhorne. Despite being anti-slavery and anti-war, many members joined the army or paid others to take their places during the Civil War. (Courtesy of the Historic Langhorne Association, Ed Vogenberger Collection.)

Built in 1931, Bowman's Hill Tower marks the observation point employed by Continental soldiers while encamped with Gen. George Washington along the Delaware River prior to their Christmas night attack on the Hessians at Trenton in 1776. The dome seen here was later struck by lightening and removed. More than 28,000 seedlings were planted on the grounds in 1932 to create Bowman's Hill State Wildflower Preserve. A Works Progress Administration project added trails in 1939. (Courtesy of Esther Smith.)

For almost two weeks during the Revolutionary War, the Moland House served as headquarters for Gen. George Washington while 11,000 Continental soldiers camped on the surrounding farmland in Warwick. The Marquis de Lafayette and Count Casimir Pulaski officially joined the American cause here. There is indication that the American flag may have been raised for the first time in the history of our country on this property. (Courtesy of the Historic Langhorne Association, Ed Vogenberger Collection.)

Emmanuel Leutze's idealized painting captures the ice-choked river, blustery cold weather, and gathering snow clouds of Christmas night, when Washington crossed the Delaware River to march on the Hessians at Trenton. The painting was loaned to Washington Crossing Historic Park on February 22, 1952, by the Metropolitan Museum of Art. Here a reproduction is prepared to replace the original before its return to the museum. (Courtesy of the Washington Crossing Historic Park, Pennsylvania Historical and Museum Commission.)

Mystery surrounds this Revolutionary War soldier's grave, as he is the only identified soldier buried in Washington Crossing Park. Commonwealth of Pennsylvania researcher Thomas A. Lainhoff found that Capt. Lt. James Moore of New York died on December 25, 1776, "after a short but excruciating fit of illness" and that Capt. Alexander Hamilton had called the 24-year-old soldier a "promising officer." Moore's tombstone was removed for safekeeping after vandals began damaging others in the county in the 1980s. (Courtesy of the Washington Crossing Historic Park, Pennsylvania Historical and Museum Commission.)

The Liberty Bell was reportedly stowed overnight in the backyard of this Quakertown home (now Liberty Hall) in 1777 while being transferred from Philadelphia to its hiding place at the Old Zion Reformed Church in Northampton Town (now Allentown). Concerned citizens and a cavalry of 200 transporting military supplies to Bethlehem had removed it for safekeeping, fearing it would be melted for musket and cannonballs by advancing British troops. (Courtesy of the Quakertown Historical Society.)

The Durner organ is among the few pipe organs of its kind in existence. The Durner Company manufactured and installed this organ in the balcony of Trumbauersville's Church of Christ in 1905. Moved to the front of the church and rededicated in 1920, it continues to serve the congregation today. (Courtesy of the Richland Library Company.)

The Willing Workers of St. Mark African Methodist Episcopal Zion Church in Newtown provided resources necessary to maintain the church building and assist the pastor. They also raised funds for Sunday school books and other needs. All were members of the Glee Club Chorus when photographed in 1928. Shown here from left to right are (first row) Howard Bainerd, Albert Shad, Clarence Gordon, William White, and Rev. Joseph Daniele; (second row) Ossie Johnson, Leroy Hopkins, James Primrose, and Booker Dingle. (Courtesy of St. Mark African Methodist Episcopal Zion Church.)

The history of Neshaminy Presbyterian Church, constructed in 1745, is intertwined with one of the world's most prestigious universities. Warminster Township historians relate that William Tennent, an early pastor who preached to Warwick's Scotch-Irish community in its original building, established Log College on York Road about 1735, "concerned about the lack of educational facilities in this new territory." Several of his ministry students later established the College of New Jersey, which became Princeton University in 1756. (Courtesy of the Historic Langhorne Association, Ed Vogenberger Collection.)

The South Perkasie Covered Bridge is the oldest covered bridge in existence in the county. Here it extends from South Main Street over the Pleasant Spring Creek in East Rockhill Township. It was later relocated to Lenape Park as a preservation measure in 1958. Signage on this well-traveled bridge warned that "smoking segars" or crossing faster than a walk risked a $5 fine! (Courtesy of Ann Bedeaux.)

Spinnerstown School in Milford Township was a two-room schoolhouse until 1952. The building now houses the Milford Township Historical Society. (Courtesy of the Richland Library Company.)

The 1855 two-story Hulmeville School accommodated 70 children. Farm work often kept pupils from the classroom, although in the fall it was filled to capacity with both adults and children. During winter, the iron stove provided barely enough heat, so girls typically added two flannel petticoats and all the children wore long underwear and leggings buttoned to the knee for warmth. Everyone brought lunch, and an old wooden pump provided water. (Courtesy of the Hulmeville Historical Society.)

The first female nominee for mayor in this part of the state was Louise Burkart. She was nominated in 1928 in one of Pennsylvania's newest boroughs, New Britain, which her husband Edwin had helped incorporate a year earlier. The oldest of nine females in her family, Louise was related to Victoria Claflin Woodhull, who in 1872 became the first woman to run for president of the United States. (Courtesy of Bruce Burkart.)

Pearl S. Buck, Bucks County author, Pulitzer Prize winner, and the first female recipient of the Nobel Prize in literature, is shown here on the left at the 1964 dedication of the Kehr Greenhouses and Orchid Collection at Delaware Valley College. In 1965, she gave the commencement address, six years before women were admitted. Buck established a successful foundation facilitating the adoption of Amerasian children. She is buried at Green Hills Farm in Perkasie, (Courtesy of the Delaware Valley College Archives.)

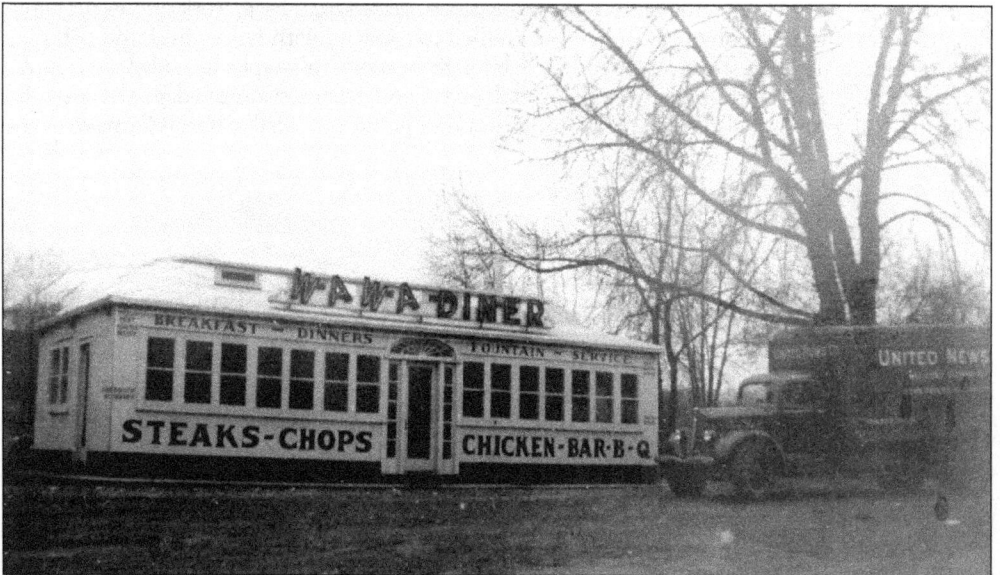

Riegelsville's WAWA Diner, started in 1939 by John DeSousa Sr., a Portuguese immigrant who arrived in 1919, was a welcome bus stop halfway between Philadelphia and Scranton. Besides helping other immigrants get established, the entrepreneurial DeSousa operated a gravel business on the nearby towpath until 1949, then a gift shop. In 1951, he converted a Doylestown home into the Farmhouse Tavern and ran it until the early 1960s. (Courtesy of Marge Blessing and Scott Blessing.)

The 24-hour Ed's Diner in Doylestown was a popular spot for over 40 years. Owner Ed Taifer worked as head cook while his wife, Laura, supervised 20 servers. Later their children Jerry and Shirley assumed Ed and Laura's respective roles. Ed's was patronized by diners of all ages, especially after high school football games in the 1950s and 1960s. On-site bakery favorites like apple dumplings with vanilla sauce kept locals saying "Meet you at Ed's!" (Courtesy of Jerry Taifer.)

Author and Pulitzer Prize winner James A. Michener visits one of his several childhood homes in Doylestown. Michener's prolific career produced over 40 books translated into more than 50 languages. The classic Rodgers and Hammerstein musical *South Pacific* was based on Michener's novel *Tales of the South Pacific* and several of his works have been adapted for film and television. Anthropologist Margaret Mead was also raised in Doylestown. (Courtesy of John Hoenstine.)

Durham Furnace supplied cannons and cannon balls to the Continental Army during the Revolution. Earlier in that century, the Durham Iron Company made cookware and stove plates with inspirational relief decorations that would line fireplaces. Around 1750, the *Durham* boat was specifically designed to transport iron ore and pig iron to mills down the Delaware River and to the Philadelphia market. (Courtesy of Gladys Koder.)

The Greenhill School was located near Lumberville. This early-20th-century photograph includes in the first row, Clarke Hendricks and Ronald Webster (third and fourth from left, respectively) and Fleury Zilli (second from right); and in the second row, Sadie Updegrove (second from left) and Dorothy Updegrove and Howard Houseley (seventh and eighth from left, respectively). Those in the third row are, from left to right, Jennie Zilli, Ted Johnson, Lester Hendricks, Maude Holcombe, Clarence Knipe, ? Winters, unidentified, ? Vasey, Margaret Wilson, Ruth Updegrove, Helen Cals, unidentified, Myrtle Hendricks, and teacher Nellie Skelton.

Established in 1877 as the Citizen's Silver Cornet Band, the Germania Band was popular at large social events and hometown parades throughout the county. According to the band's *Diamond Anniversary* retrospective, when the nation entered World War I, "it became customary to avoid anything with a hint of Germany," so the group officially became the Quakertown Band. (Courtesy of the Seifert family, the Springfield Historical Society, and Gladys Koder.)

This serene canal scene takes place at the Two Mile Lock in Edgely, Bristol Township, near the terminus of the Delaware Division of the Pennsylvania Canal. The first county borough, Bristol was home to Bucks County's first mill (1701), courthouse (1705), post office (1790), public school (1837), and telephone switchboard (1883). It was also noted throughout the country for its medicinal bath, Bath Springs, a popular resort from the 1780s to 1820s. (From the collection of the Margaret R. Grundy Memorial Library.)

The Thompson-Neely House was headquarters to Continental Army general Lord Stirling (William Alexander) in December 1776. Here Gen. George Washington and his officers discussed strategy for crossing the Delaware on Christmas night to execute the pivotal attack on Trenton. This "House of Decision," which also served as a regimental hospital for soldiers quartered in the area, is open to the public in Washington Crossing Historic Park. (Courtesy of the Washington Crossing Historic Park, Pennsylvania Historical and Museum Commission.)

The Richardson House, completed in 1738, was one of the finest in Bucks County. When built, it was rivaled only by William Penn's manor at Pennsbury and Joseph Growden's in Bensalem. Benjamin Franklin and John Hancock both visited here. Joseph Richardson moved to the village of Langhorne in 1736 upon marrying Mary Paxson. He then opened and operated the only store between Bristol and the Durham lime furnaces in Upper Bucks. (Courtesy of the Historic Langhorne Association.)

A star has been placed atop Bowman's Hill Tower every Christmas season for more than half a century by maintenance staff at Washington Crossing Historic Park to the delight of residents and travelers throughout the region. Originally the support structure for the star lights was wooden, as shown here. It is now made of steel and weighs a few hundred pounds. The men in this 1957 photograph are not identified. (Courtesy of the Washington Crossing Historic Park, Pennsylvania Historical and Museum Commission.)

The Pidcocks, shown at their 23rd family reunion in 1936, meet annually at the historic Thompson-Neely House, Gen. Lord Sterling's headquarters during the Revolutionary War. All descended from John Pidcock, one of the first whites to settle the region (his trading post used in trading with the Lenni Lenape appeared on a 1680 map). It is believed Pidcock and his wife raised their six children in the oldest portion of this home. (Courtesy of the Pidcock family.)

Fallsington's Stagecoach Tavern was rescued from deterioration through the efforts of a group of preservationists. This building and several others in the village, including a c. 1685 log home, are open for tours. William Penn, Pennsylvania's proprietor, worshiped in Fallsington and established his manor along the nearby river in Falls Township in 1682. Today Fallsington retains much of its historic past. (Courtesy of the Historic Langhorne Association, Ed Vogenberger Collection.)

The National Register of Historic Places includes these charming Colonial homes on Newtown's Court Street. William Penn's surveyor laid out Newtown in 1683–1684. It was designated county seat in 1726. During the Revolutionary War, Washington briefly established headquarters in Newtown and several noteworthy events unfolded. This was where the Committee for Safety was formed, approximately 1,000 Hessian soldiers were imprisoned, and a daring raid was perpetuated on the public treasury. (Courtesy of the Historic Langhorne Association, Ed Vogenberger Collection.)

Flannery's Restaurant in Penndel was a striking landmark at Route 1 and Durham Road for decades. Anna Flannery, who lost her husband only months after they'd opened a Parkland restaurant in 1928, purchased a building for her business at this location in 1939. Her son Jim Flannery "launched" this new look in 1967 by adding a converted Lockheed Constellation to serve as a cocktail lounge. (Courtesy of the Historic Langhorne Association.)

Cornwells firefighters pose with their new truck in 1923. Cornwells Fire Company No. 1 was chartered with 73 members on March, 21, 1915. Two years after starting with a horse-drawn engine (pulled by horses borrowed from one of its 50 members), the department bought its first motorized vehicle. It was replaced in 1921 with a Model T and then this handsome Traylor chassis. (Courtesy of the Historical Society of Bensalem.)

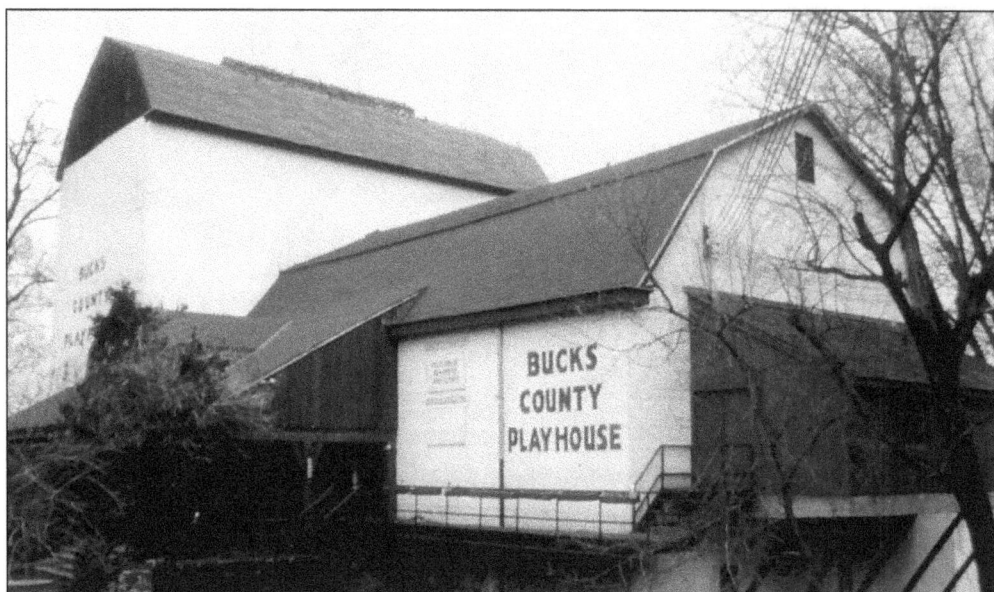

Originally a gristmill established in 1767, the Bucks County Playhouse was renovated by playwright Moss Hart and others for theatrical performances in 1939. Robert Redford, Grace Kelly, Walter Matthau, Lillian Gish, Jack Klugman, and Helen Hayes are among the notables who performed here. When late-18th-century owner Benjamin Parry lost several mills to fire, he rebuilt and renamed his business New Hope Mills, from which the surrounding village got its name. (Courtesy of the Historic Langhorne Association, Ed Vogenberger Collection.)

Deer Park Pavilion, near Solebury's Great Spring, hosted its first reunion for members of the Reorganized Church of the Latter Day Saints in July 1921. The event lasted two weeks and included an Independence Day celebration that drew more than 5,000 visitors. Opening in the 1870s to recreation and entertainment such as John Philip Sousa's band, the park had once been home to elk and buffalo and was a frequent campsite of the Lenni Lenape. (Courtesy of Esther Smith.)

Dr. Selma Burke sculpted the bronze relief plaque of Pres. Franklin D. Roosevelt that U.S. Mint engraver John Sinnock used as inspiration for the dime. Burke studied privately in Paris under celebrated artist Henri Matisse before becoming a widely known sculptress. She moved to Bucks County in 1949, where she maintained a studio for almost 50 years and founded the Bucks County Sculpture Show. (Courtesy of Ethel Gibson.)

St. Mark African Methodist Episcopal Zion Church, a source of fellowship and spiritual sustenance to Newtown's African American community since 1820, included member Dr. Selma Burke, a renowned artist who sculpted the church's unique and beautiful baptismal font. This frame building replaced two earlier structures destroyed by fire and was itself replaced by a small brick church built in 1897. A multi-cultural congregation thrives today, but long gone are the days of 5¢ oyster supper fund-raisers. (Courtesy of St. Mark African Methodist Episcopal Zion Church.)

Rohm and Haas Chemical Company, like U.S. Steel, was a major regional employer. It relocated to Bristol in 1917 on property that had once been fine meadow land. In 1807, Bela Badger owned 800 acres fronting the river here, where he operated a fish hatchery and raised race horses. This early-20th-century photograph shows Bristol in the upper left and Otter Creek skirting its way toward the Delaware River. (Courtesy of the Margaret R. Grundy Memorial Library.)

The Newtown Library Company is purported to be one of the oldest private libraries in Pennsylvania. It was established as a subscription library in 1760, and its earliest collections were maintained in the home of the librarian. Housed in a charming early-20th-century building today, the library holds over 21,000 books, many from the 18th and 19th centuries. (Courtesy of the Historic Langhorne Association, Ed Vogenberger Collection.)

The Gilbert Hicks House in Langhorne, pictured around 1880, was the 1780 birthplace of preeminent artist Edward Hicks, known for his Peaceable Kingdom paintings. It is one of four neighboring buildings once occupied by Continental soldiers after the Battle of Trenton. Nearby mass graves hold approximately 166 soldiers who died despite treatment at a hospital established by Dr. William Shippen in the village, which was then known as Four Lanes End. (Courtesy of the Historic Langhorne Association.)

Visitors to Ringing Rocks in 1914, Harry Quinby and Emma Michener sit on rocks that are part of a seven-acre boulder field in Bridgeton Township, near Bucks County's largest waterfall. These rocks ring like a bell when stuck with a hammer. Though unusual, similar fields were also formed in Springfield Township and the Stony Garden area of Haycock Township.

In this 1914 Paletown School photograph, schoolgirls appear uniformly dressed in light-colored knee-length dresses and dark stockings. A few of the boys on the right demonstrate how children once attended school barefoot. (Courtesy of the Richland Library Company.)

Durham Cave sheltered Lenni Lenape Indians for centuries and, in 1828, was the first recorded cave find in Pennsylvania. Remains of almost 50 different animals were found here. Although it was a popular early-19th-century destination, by 1850 the first two limestone chambers had been quarried out for fertilizer. This photograph shows the remaining space arranged for a July 28, 1885, meeting of the Bucks County Historical Society. (Courtesy of Marge Blessing and Scott Blessing.)

Children of Plumsteadville School proudly display their American flags and books about 1913. Built in 1858, the two-room schoolhouse was one of several in the township of Plumstead. By 1961, eight schoolhouses were available for public auction when a new elementary school was completed. (Courtesy of Ina Harmath.)

Central School, constructed in 1901 and located on Station Road near Old Bethlehem Pike, was the last one-room schoolhouse built in Richland Township. Schoolmaster Eugene Godshall strikes a rare pose while seated in front of his students. Richland Township policy in the 1850s preferred to hire male teachers for the winter months, when older farm boys could be spared from farm duties to attend school. (Courtesy of the Richland Library Company.)

The Naval Air Development Center in Warminster was an important federal military research and development facility during the second half of the 20th century. This c. 1970 view shows the base and airfield, hangars, and numerous planes. Across the center of the photograph, one can see Jacksonville Road dividing the base. Ivyland appears in the upper right. (Courtesy of Marvin Foral.)

Pvt. Howard A. Booze, great-great-uncle of Bill Harr, the present owner of Sine's Five-and-Ten Store in Quakertown, served in the Civil War with Pennsylvania's 128th Regiment, Company C. Only 19, he was killed at the Battle of Antietam on September 17, 1862, just one month after enlisting. His father was active in politics and ran for state treasurer the same year that Abraham Lincoln was seeking the presidency. (Courtesy of William Harr Sr.)

"Shiner" Walton's fife and drum band of Hulmeville and other such bands were integral to hometown parades and an exciting part of small town life in the early 1900s. Marching in a parade with one's civic group or classmates was considered an honor. Parades commemorated special occasions and public holidays throughout the year. (Courtesy of the Hulmeville Historical Society.)

The Traylor Shipyard in Bensalem Township employed 7,000 people to build wooden steamships during World War I. At the same time, the Merchant Shipbuilding Corporation in Bristol employed 12,000 workers to build merchant ships. This influx of people resulted in a new section called Harriman, named for W. Averell Harriman, owner and financier of the operation. (Courtesy of the Historical Society of Bensalem.)

Font Hill was home to archaeologist and historian Dr. Henry Mercer, who also erected the nearby Mercer Museum in Doylestown. Mercer designed both buildings and constructed them of reinforced concrete in the early 1900s. They each house an eclectic mix of historical objects he collected. Font Hill displays tiles, art, and ancient artifacts from his world travels and is located adjacent to Mercer's Moravian Pottery and Tile Works. (Courtesy of the Historic Langhorne Association, Ed Vogenberger Collection.)

Trainer's Restaurant, at Routes 309 and 313, was so popular that patrons traveled from Philadelphia and points beyond. It began by selling hot dogs, ice cream, sandwiches, fresh pies, 50¢ country ham and egg dinners, and bushels of local produce. Over time, the expansion was so significant that the closest intersection became known as Trainer's Corner. The restaurant was destroyed by fire in the 1970s. (Courtesy of the Quakertown Historical Society.)

William E. Teat began playing with the Negro League at 17 after his family moved from Maryland to Pineville in 1931. Over the next decade, Teat played with the Bucks County Tigers and Eagles, who competed against each other and against various New Jersey teams including Lambertville and Flemington. He poses with his wife, Eunice, and his son William James on Eagle Road near Jericho Mountain in the mid- to late 1930s. (Courtesy of Victor and Phyllis Teat.)

Two signers of the Declaration of Independence and Constitution sequentially owned this 18th century Morrisville home called Summerseat. Following the bankruptcy of Robert Morris, a financier of the American Revolution from whom the town derived its name, fellow signer George Clymer acquired the property. Gen. George Washington used the home as headquarters in December 1776, and two years after his inauguration in 1789, Morrisville very nearly became the nation's capital. (Courtesy of the Historic Morrisville Society.)

The Richland Library Company, established in 1788, is one of the oldest libraries in Pennsylvania. In 1795, it became the first institution chartered by the state. Stockholder and prominent patron Eleanor Foulke (seated) was actively involved in the preservation of local history. She was a founder of the women's club, a local community organization that worked for "bettering general conditions." She also served on numerous committees of the Richland Friends Meeting. (Courtesy of the Richland Library Company.)

Lulu Park's half-mile track in Quakertown, seen here around 1930, held harness races during which trained jockeys and ambitious amateurs competed to entertain patrons of the annual fair. Lulu Park also hosted the first annual Farmers Picnic in 1905. This popular affair was drawing over 10,000 people by its fifth year with events such as the Young Ladies' Hitching Contest and the 75-Yard Fat Men's Race. (Courtesy of the Quakertown Historical Society.)

Chief Strong Wolf addressed attendees on October 25, 1925, at the unveiling of a monument commemorating the historic Walking Purchase, held to claim additional land by Penn's descendants. The monument marks the meadow near Springtown where the selected walkers stopped for lunch on September 19, 1737, the first day of their one-and-a-half-day boundary-marking journey. Several Delaware Indians on that walk, suspecting fraud, left in anger near this same point. (Courtesy of Gladys Koder.)

Sarah Lukens Keene often hosted Napoleon Bonaparte's brother Joseph, the former king of Spain and Naples, at her riverfront mansion after he had fled to America following Napoleon's defeat and built a "palace" in Bordentown. Although duelers fought on the side lawn for her hand, Sarah never married. Her father refused her pleadings to wed her true love, a Philadelphia brewer. The Margaret R. Grundy Memorial Library now stands on this property. (From the collection of the Margaret R. Grundy Memorial Library.)

The Farmer's Bank of Bucks County, the first incorporated in Bucks, was started in 1814 by wealthy merchant John Hulme Jr. in Milford (which became known as Hulmeville around this time). Opening required only a seal, an iron strong-box, copper printing plates for $1, $2 and $3 bills, bank-note paper, stationery, and a ledger. In 1830, president Anthony Taylor relocated the bank to Bristol in his carriage. (Courtesy of the Hulmeville Historical Society.)

Main Street in Chalfont, leading to the Whitehall Covered Bridge, is reminiscent of a time gone by, featuring Victorian houses with a few gingerbread accents, hitching posts, a carriage stepping stone, wooden fences, and a gas lantern. James Kidd was hired about 1901 to light 30 lamps each evening for $13 a month. The borough replaced the lamps with electric lights in 1919. (Courtesy of Marilyn Becker.)

Pennsbury Manor in Falls Township fell into ruin, and the grounds were used for a time to raise corn and tobacco. As noted in an 1871 history of Bucks, it was here William Penn "sat around the Council fires of the Aborigines, and with them made enduring treaties, smoked the Calamut of peace, and inculcated the doctrine of 'Peace on earth, and good will to all men.'" In 1939, Penn's late-17th-century home was re-created and opened for tours. (Courtesy of the Historic Langhorne Association, Ed Vogenberger Collection.)

The Travel Club of Bristol commemorated George Washington's 197th birthday on February 22, 1929, by dressing in various period costumes and engaging a photographer to capture the event. The club was affiliated with the Federation of American Women's Clubs and met bimonthly. The event was held at the 1816 Keene Home, which was later replaced by the Margaret R. Grundy Memorial Library. (From the collection of the Margaret R. Grundy Memorial Library.)

Bucks County Prison, locally nicknamed "Pine Street Hotel," overlooked grounds perfect for a baseball game. The James A. Michener Art Museum, named in honor of the distinguished author and former Doylestown resident, replaced the prison in 1988. Impressionist paintings, works by woodworker George Nakashima, and an outdoor sculpture garden draw visitors from throughout the region. Mercer Museum was built on the property fronting the prison and completed in 1916. (Courtesy of the James A. Michener Art Museum Library.)

The original Anchor Tavern in Wrightstown, built in 1724 by 21-year-old Joseph Hampton, was one of the county's longest continuously operated taverns. It was destroyed by fire in July 1998. Historian George MacReynolds reported that nearby the tavern for about 50 years during the 19th century there was a wall containing the fossilized vertebrae of an extinct animal (larger than an elephant) found three miles below Buckingham Mountain around 1812. (Courtesy of Doug Crompton.)

Distinguished woodworker George Nakashima is considered "the Elder Statesman of the American Craft Movement." His exceptionally crafted furniture, influenced by both traditional Japanese and Shaker design, is showcased among the world's most important museum collections. Nakashima had been a Bucks County resident for almost 50 years before his passing in 1990. His designs are still produced at his New Hope studio, where a showroom is open to visitors. (Courtesy of the Bancroft Library, University of California Berkeley, 1967.014v.40EG-876.)

This old chemical engine was hauled out of Hulmeville's Green Street Firehouse by the William Penn Fire Company, established in 1832, for a photograph on July 9, 1927. At the reins is William K. Harrison aside William White. Others pictured from left to right are Frank Schneider, Allen C. Van Sant, Ewald Reetz, Bert Douglas (on top), Dr. Huntsman, and Abe Shaw. A donated Reading Railroad engine "tire" was used as an alarm gong. (Courtesy of the Hulmeville Historical Society.)

The Great Flood of 1955 was Mother Nature at her worst for hundreds of families along the Delaware River. Almost 200 people died. Countless homes and businesses were flooded and numerous roads and bridges were washed away. Carversville, an inland village, was also impacted. Resident and local historian Ned Harrington, who took this photograph of Bartleman's Store, recalls that "the road actually rolled up into a ball" from the water's force.

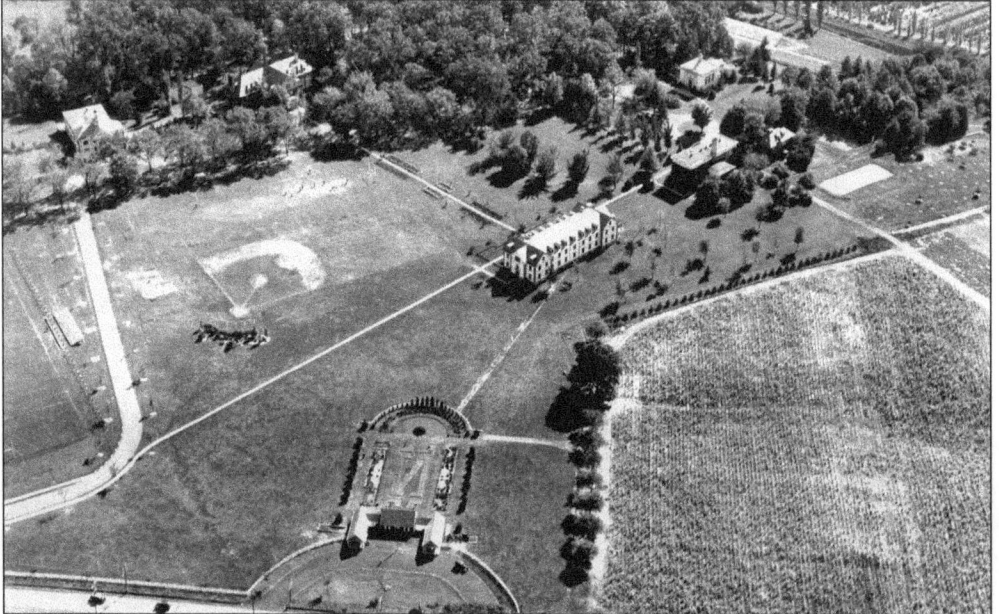

This bird's-eye view features the National Farm School in Doylestown, created as an agriculture learning center for young Jewish men "from the city." It was started in 1896 by a Philadelphian, Rabbi Joseph Krauskopf, D.D., and later became non-sectarian. The school experienced several name changes with its growth during the 20th century and has been known as Delaware Valley College since 1989. (Courtesy of the Delaware Valley College Archives.)

This 1883 Quakertown parade was photographed at Front and West Broad Streets before the train station was built. The once-prominent Bush House, shown here, was advertised in 1905 as a first class hotel with a ballroom and offered "the choicest Brandy, Wines, Liquors & Cigars." A corral to handle livestock being transported by rail to market was built adjacent to the hotel after the station was erected in 1903. (Courtesy of the Quakertown Historical Society.)

Pictured around 1900, the Stover family of Carversville included, from left to right, Helen, Amanda, Henry, Warren, Rae, and Miriam. All are descendants of Ralph Stauffer, the son of Alsace immigrants Henry and Barbara Hockman Stauffer. Ralph changed his name to Stover while serving as a member of the state assembly from 1793 to 1799. By 1850, Stover family members owned several grist- and sawmills in the Tohickon area, which was called Stovertown until 1872.

Tyro Hall School in Mechanicsville was the second so named in Buckingham Township's Tyron School District. An earlier school, built about 1790 on Holicong Road below Mechanicsville Road, was academically outstanding. An early student later recalled it being situated among woods, springs, and a stream one mile from "a grove of very excellent sweet birch." His Irish schoolmasters used Murray's *English Reader*, Bonnycastle's *Algebra*, Pike's *Arithmetic*, Comly's *Spelling*, and Gummere's *Surveying* to teach their young scholars. (Courtesy of Glenn Dutterer.)

Richlandtown Primary School students pose with their teacher, Emma Price, on January 22, 1903. A Victorian reed organ shown in a later classroom photograph (1905) was perhaps state of the art for that time and could be purchased through the Sears Roebuck and Company catalogue. A new school, built on Church Street in 1909, replaced this 1855 facility on Route 212. (Courtesy of the Richland Library Company.)

Sine's Five-and-Ten Store, a Quakertown establishment since 1912, remains a nostalgic gateway to the past and a unique shopping experience after almost 100 years. This photograph captures the grand opening of a building addition in 1937. Sine's is the last five-and-dime in the region and still carries a wide variety of hard-to-find items, offers 32 varieties of penny candy, and serves breakfast and lunch at its soda fountain. (Courtesy of William Harr Sr.)

The New Britain Baptist Church was erected in 1744. It "stood in the midst of a fine bit of virgin forest" to serve Welsh settlers, according to 19th-century historian Edward Matthews. An enlarged model of the original 30-by-40-foot building was erected through donations of timber, money, and labor in 1812. The east end was expanded in 1857, and the chapel was added in 1884. American Indians are believed to be buried in churchyard graves marked by stones. (Courtesy of Bruce Burkart.)

The 1878 courthouse was located on the site of Doylestown's first facility (opened in 1812 with an adjoining jailhouse) on lands donated by Nathaniel Shewell. Doylestown became the county seat in 1810 when it was moved there from Newtown. This second courthouse was demolished, along with the administration building, when the present structure was erected in 1960. A Civil War monument dedicated to the 104th Regiment remains nearby. (Courtesy of the Historic Langhorne Association, Ed Vogenberger Collection.)

The Springtown Hotel was built around 1830 by Christopher Witte, who served as local postmaster during Andrew Jackson's administration. According to David Cressman in 1891, the hotel competed with the White Horse Tavern until "Witte's house got the stronger hold on the public." Pictured here about 1900 is the Muhelheiser family of Quakertown. (Courtesy of Gladys Koder.)

Augustus Schuler, proprietor of a hotel in Milford Township, started Schuler's Cornet Band of Finland in the 1880s. Shown here around 1901 is 18-year-old Sarah Pfaff, the conductor and only woman in the band. Members included four of her brothers: Lewis, Calvin, Horace, and Fred. Milton Pfaff, Sarah's father, once served as conductor also. The band lasted 20 years. (Courtesy of the Richland Library Company.)

Mount Gilead African Methodist Episcopal Church, built in 1852, provided shelter and solace to fugitive slaves traveling the Underground Railroad. A small black community settled on Buckingham Mountain formed a congregation there as early as 1822. These residents built their first church, a log structure, in 1834 and hosted camp meetings attended by their white neighbors. Today the building is maintained in that same spirit of community by a group of dedicated local volunteers. (Sketch by Richard Pullinger; courtesy of Kathryn Auerbach.)

Quakertown Farmers Market began in 1932 as a family goods auction on the farm of Stanley Rotenberger. When the Woldow family took over in the 1940s, it was a thriving indoor/outdoor market. Going to the market was as much a social event as a necessity, and attracted 50,000 weekend shoppers in the 1950s. Today thousands of shoppers continue to visit. (Courtesy of John Chism.)

The Springtown Post Office was established in 1806. This photograph, taken 101 years later, shows postmistress Anna Fluck Sweigard and the town's first mail carriers with their horse-and-buggy delivery wagons. Henry D. Cressman (left) was responsible for Rural Free Delivery Route No. 2 and Bill Weamer (right) handled No. 1. The other two men are not identified. (Courtesy of Ruth Johnson.)

This eight-arch Pennsylvania Railroad bridge carries a steam locomotive over the Neshaminy Creek around 1935. This area is presently known as Playwicki Park. A Native American "town," referenced in a 1683 letter by William Penn as "Playwicken," is thought to have been located in the vicinity. Historian George MacReynolds noted that the name is a corruption of a Lenni Lenape word meaning "the place which is full of turkeys." (Courtesy of the Historic Langhorne Association.)

The Mercer Museum in Doylestown was built of concrete and contained 33 fireproof rooms and 36 alcoves when completed in 1916. The original exhibits of founder Dr. Henry Chapman Mercer, an archeologist and historian, displayed objects "used in agriculture, industry and the home up to 1820, or until the introduction of steam & modern machinery." (Courtesy of the Historic Langhorne Association, Ed Vogenberger Collection.)

Samuel Strunk founded Strunk's Funeral Home in Quakertown and was succeeded by his son Ruben, and later by his daughter-in-law Sarah. Pictured here at the Strunk family reunion around 1900 from left to right are (first row) Johannes Strunk and Carolina Strunk (née Weaver), Kate Knapp (née Strunk), Mary Clymer (née Strunk), Henry Harwick and Susan Harwick (née Strunk), Samuel Taylor and Elizabeth Taylor (née Strunk), and Samuel Renner and Lydia Renner (née Strunk); (second row) Reuben Strunk and Sarah Strunk (née Musselman), Henry Strunk and Ann Strunk (née Hoffert), William Braucher and Katie Braucher (née Strunk), Samuel Strunk and Elizabeth Strunk (née Roth), and Henry Heist and Leanna Heist (née Strunk). (Courtesy of William Harr Sr.)